Master Minds 60s & 70s
Rock & Roll Quiz Book
Volume 2

Another year's worth of weekly quizzes

By Kevin Taggart

Copyright © Kevin Taggart
The right of Kevin Taggart to be identified as the Author of this work has been asserted by him in accordance with the Copyright, Design, and Patents Act 1988.

A CIP catalogue for this book is available from the British Library.

Introduction

Another year of 52 quizzes!

Last year I published a music quiz book featuring 52 quizzes that I set to members of my Facebook Music Page in a weekly quiz. Such is the popularity of my quizzes that I have now enough material to compile another book of quizzes that you can use in various ways – either in a club, in a pub, or in a quiz in your own house with a few friends.

One change from last year's book is that I now set 20 questions per quiz as opposed to 15 questions last year. Each quiz ends with a bonus question that's a little more difficult than the rest, but which I give double points for a correct answer.

With almost 1,100 questions and answers you'll never be stuck for a music quiz either in your home or down the pub!

All chart questions apply to the U.K. Charts.

[Answers are given at the rear of the book.]

Thanks

Once again, I'm indebted to Joe McCoubrey for his proofreading, editing, and formatting of this book. Joe has been editing my various category of books since 2013. He gives his time and effort without question and has helped me enormously these past ten years.

Joe is a talented novelist, and his thriller books are among the best in the genre. I wholeheartedly recommend each one of his novels.

Dedication

A special word of praise to the Big Boss, Annie Amos, who oversees the smooth running of our Facebook group. Annie is an old hand in the running of such a group and her expertise, knowledge, and keen sense of humour means that our members can partake in posting their various favourite videos, take part in my quizzes, enjoy charts from our timeline and enter Annie's 'Theme Days' to relive the golden age of rock and pop music.

To "My Dream Band of Quizzers" who week after week show their prowess in the knowledge of the golden age of Rock & Roll.

Among my regular group are Dan, Bob, Katharine, Mike, Geoffrey, Roger, Mandy, Catherine, Brian, Simon, Danny, Jennie, Jane, Rose, and Paul.

QUIZ NUMBER 1

1. "Let it Bleed" was a number 1 hit album in 1969/1970 for what group?

2. "Philadelphia Freedom " was a top twenty hit single for what singer/songwriter in 1975?

3. What legendary singer had a 1969 hit single with "Love's Been Good to Me?"

4. Yvonne Elliman had a top five hit single in 1978 with "If I Can't Have -". What's the missing word in the title?

5. Freda Payne was a one hit wonder on the U.K. Charts. Can you name her 1970 number 1 hit single?

6. What was the Casuals only top ten hit single?

7. The Top 3 acts of 1966 were (1) The Beach Boys, (2) The Spencer Davis Group. Can you name the third bestselling act that year?

8. Who wrote Badfinger's debut hit single, "Come and Get It" in 1969?

9. From what number 1 hit single in 1972 do the following lyrics appear?
"Now, I understand what you tried to say to me
And how you suffered for your sanity
And how you tried to set them free
They would not listen, they did not know how
Perhaps they'll listen now."

4

10. "Off the Wall" was a top 5 hit album for what singer/songwriter in 1979?

11. Who was the original lead guitarist with the rock group, Free?

12. How many number 1 solo hit singles did Marvin Gaye have in the 1960's and 1970's. One, Two, or Three?

13. Pauline Matthews, born in Bradford in 1947, achieved fame when she changed her name to what?

14. What country singer recalled a gypsy woman in his top 30 hit single in 1976?

15. In what city did Dusty Springfield record her 1969 hit single, "Son of a Preacher Man?"

16. Who sang lead vocals on 10cc's "I'm Mandy, Fly Me" hit single in 1976?

17. In the singles charts, week ending 19th August 1965, The Byrds had two Songs in the top twenty both written by Bob Dylan. One song was "Mr Tambourine Man." Can you name the other?

18. "Daydreamer"/"The Puppy Song" was a number 1 hit single in 1973 for what singer?

19. What did the clown say in a 1967 hit single for Manfred Mann?

20. Whose covers album called "Pin-Ups was a number 1 hit in 1973?

Bonus Question:
Peter Alexander Greenlaw Kinnes was the bassist - from 1963 to 1969 - in what top group?

QUIZ NUMBER 2

1. 10 cc had a top ten hit single in 1973 with "The Dean and -". What's the missing word in the title?

2. "Meaty, Beaty, Big and Bouncy" was a top ten hit album for what group in 1971?

3. The Kinks had one number 1 hit single in 1965. Can you name the song?

4. What singer's backing group was called the Pips?

5. On what record label was the George Harrison's "My Sweet Lord" single released on?

6. In what year did Paul Jones leave Manfred Mann?

7. On what famous number 1 hit single do the following lyrics appear?
" Mama,
Just killed a man,
Put a gun against his head, pulled my trigger,
Now he's dead."

8. What number did Dusty Springfield count to in her top ten hit single in 1968?

9. "Sir Duke" was a top 5 hit single for what singer/songwriter in 1977?

10. Chris Andrews had a couple of solo hit singles in 1965, but what singer did he write six top twenty hit singles for in 1965 and 1966?

11. "Never Let Her Slip Away " was a hit single in 1978 for what singer/songwriter?

12. "Rainbow Valley" was the follow-up single to what number 1 hit by the Love Affair in 1968?

13. "Have You Seen Her?" was a hit single in early 1972 for what group?

14. "Young Americans" was a hit album and single for what singer/songwriter in 1975?

15. Who was lead singer with The Dave Clark Five?

16. Roy Wood wrote three number 1 hit singles, one in the 1960's and two in the 1970's. Can you name any one of the three?

17. "Ballroom Blitz" was a top 3 hit single for what group in 1973?

18. "Smiley Smile" was a top ten hit album in 1967 for what group?

19. Who was lead singer/guitarist with Dire Straits?

20. Did Ringo Starr have a number 1 hit single in the 1970's?

Quiz 2 Bonus Question
Tom Jones had a top ten hit single in 1967 with a four-word titled song. Each word begins with the same letter. Can you name the hit?

QUIZ NUMBER 3

1. "That Same Old Feeling" was a top five hit single on the charts for Picketywitch in 1970. Who was the group's lead singer?

2. "Willy and the Poor Boys" was a 1970 hit album for what group?

3. Paul Simon's "*59th Street Bridge Song (Feelin' Groovy")* was a minor hit for what group in 1967?

4. What was Manfred Mann's Earth Band blinded by in its hit single in 1976?

5. *"Cold Turkey"* was a 1969 hit for what band?

6. From what number 1 hit single do the following lyrics appear?
"The mornin' sun when it's in your face really shows your age
But that don't worry me none, in my eyes, you're everything
I laughed at all of your jokes, my love, you didn't need to coax."

7. Who had a hit single in 1961 with *"Hit the Road Jack"*?

8. What singer had a hit single in 1971 with Carole King's "You've Got a Friend."?

9. *"The Wall"* was a hit album in 1979 for what rock

group?

10. *"Got to Get You into my life"* was a hit single for Cliff Bennett and the Rebel Rousers in 1966. What Beatles album was the song on?

11. "Skweeze Me Pleeze Me" was a number 1 hit single in 1973 for what group?......(Slade)

12. Three world class guitarists were - at separate times - members of the Yardbirds. The name of two were Jeff Beck and Eric Clapton. Can you name the third?

13. In what year in the 1960's was "Something in the Air " by Thunderclap Newman a number 1 hit single?

14. Don Fardon had a 1970 hit single with "Indian - ". What's the missing word in the title?

15. Who produced "Don't Answer Me" a hit single for Cilla Black in 1966?

16. "Tell Me When" was a 1964 hit single for what group?

17. What group had a 1968 hit single called "I Don't Want Our Loving to Die?"

18. "Does Your Mother Know" was a hit single in 1979 for what group?

19. Ringo Starr had a 1971 hit single with "It Don't Come - ". What's the missing word in the title?

20. "Sha La La" was a hit single in 1964, "Sha La La La Lee" was a hit single in 1966. Which song was a hit for Manfred Mann?

Bonus Question:
George Martin played different instruments on many Beatles album tracks and singles. Do you know how many songs he played on?

QUIZ NUMBER 4

1. "Breakfast in America" was a top 3 album in 1979 for what group?

2. What was the Turtles second top twenty hit single in the UK charts?

3. "I Don't Like Mondays" was a number 1 hit single for what group in 1979?

4. "He's in Town" was a hit single for the Rockin' Berries in 1964. What famous couple wrote the song?

5. "The Twelfth of Never" was covered by many acts, but who took the song to number 1 in the singles chart in March 1973?

6. From what classic number 1 hit single do these lyrics appear?
"If her daddy's rich, take her out for a meal
If her daddy's poor, just do what you feel
Speed along the lane, do a ton or a ton and twenty-five."

7. In the singles chart in early 1968 what type of bush was the group Traffic going around?

8. America's answer to The Beatles had a number 2 hit album in 1967 called "Headquarters." Can you name the group?

9. Where were Martha and the Vandellas dancing in their 1964 hit single?

10. What group had a top 5 hit single in 1971 with "No Matter What?"

11. Did the Rolling Stones "Let's Spend the Night Together"/"Ruby Tuesday " reach the top of the charts in 1967?

12. Who was lead singer with Mud?

13. Who did Marv Johnson pick a rose for in his 1969 top ten hit single?

14. What group had a hit single in 1979 with Eddie Cochrane's "Something Else?"

15. What Welsh group's debut hit single was "Gin House" in 1967?

16. What time was it according to Faron Young in his 1972 top ten single?

17. Who was lead singer with The Jam?

18. Two singers were on the wrong side of the law in the chart ending 12th.June 1971. One was at number 2 with "I Did What I Did for Maria" and the other was at number 3 with "Indiana Wants Me ". Can you name both singers?

19. In what year was the New York Mining Disaster according to the Bee Gees in their debut hit single in 1967?

20. On what river was Gerry and the Pacemakers taking a ferry on in their 1965 hit single?

Bonus Question:
Who sang lead vocals on the Moody Blues 1965 number 1 hit single "Go Now"?

QUIZ NUMBER 5

1. "The More I See You" was a top 5 hit single in 1966 for what singer?

2. "Red Light Spells -" was a hit for Billy Ocean in 1977. What's the missing word in the title?

3. "Aladdin Sane" was a number 1 hit album for what singer/songwriter in 1973?

4. Who took Tony Jackson's place in the Searchers in 1964?

5. "Angel" was a top ten hit single for Rod Stewart in 1972. Who wrote the song?

6. "Holy Cow" was a top ten hit single for what soul singer in 1966?

7. Were any of the Walker Brothers real brothers?

8. From what classic hit do the following lyrics appear?
"You know that a man ain't supposed to cry
But these tears I can't hold inside
Losin' you would end my life you see
'Cause you mean that much to me."

9. What type of holiday had 10cc in its number 1 single in 1978?

10. What legendary American group had a hit album in 1970 with "Sunflower?"

11. How many drunken nights did the Dubliners have in their 1967 top ten hit single?

12. Who did Dandy Livingstone warn Suzanne to be beware of in his top 20 hit single in 1972?

13. "Come and Stay with Me" was a top 20 hit for what singer in 1965?

14. "Sugar Baby Love " was a number 1 hit single in 1974 for what group?

15. What's the total number in this question?
(1) The number of trombones in a song from the musical "The Music Man"in 1962.....(2) the number in the act that had a top ten hit single in 1968 with Bob Dylan's "This Wheel's On Fire.......(3) the number of times Dawn knocked in their hit in 1971......(4) the total number in a hit by Len Barry in 1965. (5) the number that Pete Wingfield sang about in his hit single in 1975?

16. Dave Davies sang about the death of who in his 1967 top 5 hit single?

17. Was the single "Hotel California" a number 1 hit in the U.K for the Eagles?

18. What group was down the dust pipe in its top 20 hit single in 1970?

19. Who had a hit album with "Extra Texture (Read All About it") in 1975?

20. "The Israelites " was originally a number 1 hit single in 1969. It was re-released and became a hit again in 1975. Who recorded the single?

Bonus Question:
"Dead End Street " was the original title of which ELO track on its 1977 "Out of The Blue" album?

QUIZ NUMBER 6

1. What jazz musician played the tenor saxophone solo on the Beatles "Lady Madonna "single?

2. What group had a top 20 hit album in 1970 with "Morrison Hotel?"

3. "Hello Suzie" was a top 5 hit single for what group in 1969?

4. Don Felder and what other guitarist played on the outro of the Eagles "Hotel California" single?

5. Vanilla Fudge had a hit single in 1967 with a song that was first made famous by the Supremes. Can you name the song?

6. "Watching the Detectives" was a hit single in 1977 for what act?

7. "All the Way to Memphis" was a hit single for what group in 1973?

8. "The Resurrection -" was a 1971 hit single for Ashton, Gardiner, and Dyke. What's the missing word in the song title?

9. From which classic hit do the following lyrics appear?
"You've got a lotta nerve to say you are my friend
When I was down you just stood there grinnin'
You've got a lotta nerve to say you got a helping hand to lend

10. "Killing Me Softly with His Song" was a 1973 hit single for what American singer?

11. Who produced "River Deep Mountain High" for Ike and Tina Turner?

12. What group had a number 1 hit single in 1975 with "January?

13. What singer recorded the original version of "The Sun Ain't Gonna Shine Anymore?"

14. Who was lead singer with Roxy Music?

15. Honeybus had one top ten single in 1968. Can you name the song?

16. What Country singer, who died in 1964, had a top 5 hit album in that year with "Moonlight and Roses?"

17. "Gudbuy T'jane" was a hit single in 1973 for what group?

18. B.J. Thomas sang the original version of "Mama". Who had a top ten hit single with the song in the UK charts in the summer of 1966?

19. "Betcha by Golly, wow" was a 1972 hit single for what group?

20. "Be Young, Be Foolish, Be Happy" was a minor hit in 1970 for what group?

Bonus Question:

Three-part question. Two points for each correct answer:

Cissy Houston, Doris Troy, Dionne Warwick, and Dee Dee Warwick sang backing vocals on a 1961 single that was covered by a Liverpool group two years later. (1) Name the song (2) Name the original act that first recorded it and (3) Name the Liverpool group that recorded the song in 1963?

QUIZ NUMBER 7

1. Renaldo "Obie" Benson was a member of which Motown group?

2. What prolific hit making group had a top ten hit single in 1965 with "Yes I Will"?

3. From what classic hit do the following lyrics appear?
"I've got so much honey
The bees envy me
I've got a sweeter song
Than the birds in the trees
Well, I guess you'd say
What can make me feel this way?"

4. "New Boots and Panties" was a 1977 hit album for what act?

5. Another prolific hit making group had a top ten single in 1966 with "Hideaway". Can you name the group?

6. "Turn to Stone" was released as a single from which ELO album in 1977?

7. "High Time" was the debut hit single in 1966 for what singer?

8. "Still Crazy After All These Years" was a 1975 hit album and single for which singer/songwriter?

9. "Goodbye to Love" was a 1972 hit single for what act?

10. Who had a 1969 hit single with "Windmills of Your Mind?"

11. What type of butterfly did Bob Lind sing about in his hit single in 1966?

12. What number do you get when you add the number of steps to Heaven (Eddie Cochrane) the number of days in the week, (the Beatles), the many times a lady, (The Commodores), the number of nervous breakdowns (The Rolling Stones), and the number of ways to leave your lover, (Paul Simon)?

13. Who played bass on George Harrison's 1973 hit single, "Give Me Love (Give Me Peace on Earth)?

14. "The Son of Hickory Holler's Tramp" was a 1968 hit single for what singer?

15. Unit 4 + 2 had a 1965 number 1 single with "Concrete and Clay. What American singer covered the song in 1976 and had a number 11 hit with it in the UK charts?

16. Was "I Say a Little Prayer" by Aretha Franklin a hit in the UK charts in 1968?

17. Who had a number 1 hit single with "I Hear You Knocking " in 1970?

18. In what city was folk singer Donovan born?

19. "Atlantic Crossing" was a 1975 hit album for what singer/songwriter?

20. Who wrote "Walk on By" for Dionne Warwick?

Bonus Question:
We've all heard of the phrase "Teen Idol", but what singer was it coined for?

QUIZ NUMBER 8

1. "No Particular Place to Go" was a 1964 hit single for what singer/songwriter?

2. "The Night Has a Thousand Eyes" was a hit for what singer in 1962?

3. Carl Wayne was lead singer with what group in the late 1960s?

4. What Motown group had a hit with "My Girl"?

5. From what classic hit of 1969 do the following lyrics appear?
"Hand out the arms and ammo
We're going to blast our way through here
We've got to get together sooner or later
Because the revolution's here, and you know it's right"?

6. "Time is Tight" was a 1968 hit single for what famous Memphis group?

7. Who was lead singer with the Derry group, The Undertones?

8. What is the famous rock opera Pete Townsend began writing in 1968?

9. What are/were the surnames of the duo, Peter, and Gordon?

10. "Everything's Tuesday" was a hit single in 1971 for what group?

11. Who was lead singer with the Fortunes in the hit making years?

12. Who was the drummer with The Move in the late 1960s and early 1970s before becoming a member of ELO?

13. "One of These nights" was a hit album and single for what group in 1975?

14. Who was lead singer with Black Sabbath?

15. "Crime of the Century" was a hit album for what group in 1974?

16. In what city were the Animals formed?

17. What group had a hit with "Money, Money, Money" in 1976?

18. What singer/songwriter had a hit album in 1975 with "Still Crazy After All These Years"?

19. "My Sweet Lord" was a monster hit single for George Harrison in 1971. What album was the classic taken off?

20. In what year did "Maggie May" top the singles chart for Rod Stewart?

Quiz 8 Bonus Question. "Itchycoo Park" was a 1967 hit single for what group?

QUIZ NUMBER 9

1. Who was lead singer with the Four Tops?

2. "Come Back and Shake Me" was a 1969 hit single for what Northern Irish singer?

3. "Goodbye Stranger" by Supertramp came off which 1979 album?

4. What legendary group recorded the album, "Holland" in 1973?

5. "It's Magic" was a hit single for what Scottish group in 1974?

6. Who replaced Florence Ballard in the Supremes in 1967?

7. "Ooh La La" was a hit single for the Faces in 1973. Who sang lead vocals on the song?

8. Peter Green was lead guitarist and lead singer with what group in the late 1960s?

9. "The tracks of my Tears" was a hit single in 1969 for what group?

10. Eric Clapton, Jack Bruce, and who else were members of the rock group, Cream?

11. Did "Waterloo Sunset" by the Kinks top the charts in 1967?

12. Who sang lead vocals on 10cc's 1975 number 1 hit single, "I'm Not in Love"?

13. Gerry and the Pacemakers first three singles went to number 1 on the charts. They are, "How Do You Do It", "I Like It", and what other song?

14. "Metal Guru" was the final number 1 hit single for what group in 1972?

15. Who was the drummer with the Jimi Hendrix Experience?

16. From what classic hit do the following lyrics appear?
"Ah you never turned around to see the frowns
On the jugglers and the clowns when they all did tricks for you
You never understood that it ain't no good
You shouldn't let other people get your kicks for you".

17. On what Beatles album does "I'm Only Sleeping" appear?

18. "Yellow River" was a 1970 number 1 hit single for what group?

19. "Rat Trap" was a 1978/1979 hit single for what group?

20. "Are You Lonesome Tonight " was a 1960 number 1 for what singer?

Bonus Question: Who recorded the original version of "The End of The World"?

QUIZ NUMBER 10

1. "The More I See You" was a 1966 hit single for what American singer?

2. What punk group had a 1977 hit with "God Save the Queen"?

3. Al Green had a 1971 hit single with "Tired of Being - ". What's the missing word in the title?

4. Who had a number 2 hit single in 1969 with "I'm Gonna Make You Mine?"

5. Who was the 'Delta Lady' in the song written by Leon Russell and recorded by Joe Cocker?

6. "Sylvia's Mother" was the debut hit single for what American group in 1972?

7. Who was the original bassist in The Who?

8. "Eighteen with a Bullet" was a top ten hit single for what singer in 1975?

9. Who was lead singer with Free and Bad Company?

10. The group Hotlegs - that had a 1970 hit single with "Neanderthal Man - morphed into what popular group in 1972?

11. What were/are the forenames of The Carpenters?

12. "She'd Rather Be with Me " was a hit for the Turtles in what year?

13. "Are You Experienced" was a 1967 hit album for what group?

14. "A Night on the Town" was a hit album in 1976 for what singer/songwriter?

15. Who was lead singer with Blondie?

16. Did the Eagles have a number 1 hit album in the UK in the 1970's?

17. "Endless Flight" was a hit album for what singer in 1976?

18. In what classic hit do the following lyrics appear?
"I had nothing to do on this hot afternoon
But to settle down and write you a line
I've been meaning to phone you but from Minnesota
Hell, it's been a very long time?"

19. "Distant Drums" was a number 1 hit single in 1966 for what Country star?

20. Paul and Barry Ryan had a 1965 hit single with "Have Pity on The -". What's the missing word in the title?

Bonus Question: What was Gilbert O'Sullivan's debut hit single in 1970?

QUIZ NUMBER 11

1. Who discovered the singer Mary Hopkin and signed her to the 'Apple label in 1968?

2. "Silk Degrees" was a 1976 hit album for what singer/songwriter?

3. Was "My Sweet Lord" by George Harrison a number 1 hit single?

4. "Deja Vu" was a hit album for what group in 1970?

5. Who sang lead vocals on the Beach Boys 1965 hit single "Help Me Rhonda" ?

6. "Juliet" was a 1964 number 1 hit single for what group?

7. Who was the drummer with Slade?

8. What song was the Kinks first number 1 hit in 1964?

9. "Pearl's A Singer" was a 1977 for what singer?

10. In what year was "Silence is Golden" a number 1 hit single for The Tremeloes?

11. "Get Down" was a 1973 number 1 hit single for what singer/songwriter?

12. Long John Baldry had one number 1 hit single in our timeframe. Can you name it?

13. "Mercy Mercy Me" was a hit single for Marvin Gaye in 1971. What album did the song come off?

14. Who sang lead vocals on "Loving Things," the debut hit for The Marmalade in 1968?

15. From what famous 1979 hit single do the following lyrics appear?
"Hong Kong is up for grabs
London is full of Arabs
We could be in Palestine
Overrun by the Chinese line
With the boys from the Mersey and the Thames and the Tyne".

16. What singer had a 1969 hit single with "Dizzy?"

17. "Seasons in the Sun" was a 1974 number 1 hit single for what singer?

18. Which two Beatles didn't play on the group's 1969 number 1 hit, "The Ballad of John and Yoko"?

19. "Fanfare for The Common Man" was a 1977 hit single for what group?

20. The 1965 PJ Proby hit single; "Maria" came from which famous musical?

Bonus Question:

The (B) side of the Applejack's 1964 hit "Tell Me When" was a song called "Baby Jane" written by Pete Dello and Ray Cane. Four years later, the duo formed a group that had a top ten hit single. Can you name the group and the hit?

QUIZ NUMBER 12

1. The Easybeats had a top ten hit single in 1966 with "Friday on My -". Can you name the missing word in the title?

2. "A Gift from a Flower to a Garden" was a hit album in 1968 for what singer/songwriter?

3. "Sugar Baby Love" was a 1974 number 1 hit single for what group?

4. Wilson Pickett had a top 30 hit in 1969 with his version of what Beatles number 1 hit single from the previous year?

5. From what classic hit do the following lyrics appear?
"But if you leave me a hundred times
A hundred times I'll take you back
I'm yours whenever you want me
I'm not too proud to shout it, tell the world about it"?

6. "Gasoline Alley " was a 1970 album for what singer/songwriter?

7. Who was the lead singer with Wizzard?

8. The Lemon Pipers had one top ten hit single in 1968 with what song?

9. Who was lead singer with Mott the Hoople?

10. "We Gotta Get Out of This Place" by The Animals was kept off the top of the charts by which Beatles single in 1965?

11. Who was lead singer with The Supremes after Diana Ross left for a solo career?

12. "Car Wash" was a 1977 hit single for what group?

13. The Tremeloes "Here Comes My Baby, a hit single in 1967, was written by what singer/songwriter?

14. "The Original Soundtrack" was a 1975 hit album by what group?

15. Blue Weaver was keyboardist with The Strawbs in the 1970s before playing with the Bee Gees for many years. What 1960's group did he first achieve success?

16. "Sunday Girl" was a number 1 hit single in 1979 for what group?

17. Who took Bernie Leadon's place in the Eagles in 1975?

18. "Glass of Champagne" was a number 1 hit single in 1976 for what group?

19. "Love is All Around" was a 1967 hit single for the Troggs. Who wrote the song?

20. In what city is The Doors lead singer, Jim Morrison buried?

Quiz 12 Bonus Question:

Status Quo had only one number 1 hit single in our timeframe. Can you name the song?

QUIZ NUMBER 13

1. "Pisces, Aquarius, Capricorn, & Jones Ltd" was a 1967 hit album by what group?

2. Chris Norman was the lead singer with what group in the 1970's?

3. "Last Night in -" was a 1968 top ten single for Dave Dee, Dozy, Beaky, Mick, and Tich. What's the missing word in the title?

4. "Never Let Her Slip Away" was a top ten hit single in 1978 for what singer?

5. Oliver had a 1969 hit single with a song from the musical 'Hair'. Can you name the hit?

6. From what classic hit do the following lyrics appear?
"Well, the undertaker drew a heavy sigh
Seeing no one else had come
And a bell was ringing in the village square
For the rabbits on the run"?

7. "I Was Made to Love Her" was a 1967 hit single for what singer?

8. "How Do You Like It" was a 1963 hit album for what group?

9. What was The Troggs debut top twenty hit single?

10. What singer had a number 1 hit single with "Sailing" in 1975?

11. "Goodbye to Love" was a 1972 hit single for what duo?

12. "She'd Rather Be with Me" was a hit single for what group in 1967?

13. From what classic hit do the following lyrics appear?
" Don't question why she needs to be so free
She'll tell you it's the only way to be
She just can't be chained
To a life where nothing's gained
And nothing's lost, at such a cost"?

14. "Life is a Minestrone " was a 1975 hit single for what group?

15. What was Gary Puckett's backing band called?

16. In what year did the Beatles have its first hit single, "Love Me Do"?

17. Who is/was the drummer with Queen?

18. "You Don't Bring Me -" was a hit single for Neil Diamond and Barbara Streisand in 1978. What's the missing word in the title?

19. What was Don McLean's debut hit single?

20. Which duo wrote "Alfie", a hit for Cilla Black in 1966?

Bonus Question:
Marmalade had a number 1 hit single with The Beatles, "Ob-La-Di Ob-La-Da" in January 1969. What other group took its version into the top 20 at the same time?

QUIZ NUMBER 14

1. Steve Winwood was in three famous bands in the 1960s.....They were, The Spencer Davis Group...... Traffic..... Can you name the third?

2. How many number 1 hit singles did the Small Faces have?

3. In what year did "Bridge Over Troubled Water" top the UK singles charts?

4. What was ABBA's first number 1 hit single?

5. Who produced ELO's "Out of the Blue" album, released in 1977?

6. "Part of the Union" was a 1973 hit single for what group?

7. From what classic song do the following lyrics appear?
"You know I've seen a lot of what the world can do
And it's breakin' my heart in two
Because I never wanna see you sad, girl
Don't be a bad girl."

8. "Walls and Bridges" was a 1974 hit album for what legendary singer/songwriter?

9. "Piper at the Gates of Dawn" was a 1967 hit album for what group?

10. "Indiana Wants Me" was a 1971 hit single for what singer?

11. "My Eyes Adored You" was a hit single for what veteran singer in 1975?

12. John Lodge was bassist with what group whose hit singles include "Question" in 1970 and "Isn't Life Strange" in 1972?

13. "A Day Without Love" written by Phillip Goodhand-Tait was a hit single for what group in 1968?

14. "All Things Must Pass" was a hit album for what ex-Beatle in 1971?

15. "Hurdy Gurdy Man" was a hit single for what singer/songwriter in 1968?

16. Who was the drummer with Blondie?

17. Which Monkee sang lead vocals on "Alternate Title" in 1967?

18. "Oh! No Not My Baby" written by Gerry Goffin and Carole King was a hit in 1965 for Manfred Mann. The song went into the charts again in 1973, but who had a hit with it then?

19. "Private Number" was a 1968 hit single for William Bell and what female soul singer?

20. "Ooh La La" was a hit album for what group in 1973?

Bonus Question:
Which album was the Rolling Stones last number 1 in the 1970's?

QUIZ NUMBER 15

1. What group had a 1973 hit album with "Quadrophenia?"

2. "Take Good Care of My Baby" was a 1962 hit single for what American singer?

3. Jim Capaldi had a hit single in 1975 with what song that was originally a hit for the Everly Brothers in 1960?

4. "Can You Please Crawl Out Your Window?" was a top twenty hit single in 1966 for what folk singer turned rock star?

5. The Patti Smith Group had a 1978 hit single with "Because the Night." Who wrote the song along with Patti?

6. When Keith Moon died, who took his place as the drummer with The Who?

7. "Strawberry Fields Forever" and what other song gave the Beatles a number 2 hit single in February 1967?

8. Eric Carmen had a 1976 hit single with "All By - ". What's the missing word in the title?

9. From what classic hit do the following lyrics appear?
*"I suppose I could collect my books and get on back to school
Or steal my daddy's cue and make a living out of playin' pool*

*Or find myself a rock and roll band that needs a helpin'
hand"?*

10. Where were The Police walking on in their hit single
of 1979?

11. "Make it With You" was a 1970 number 5 hit single
for what group?

12. Who was the drummer with the Kinks from 1964 to
1984?

13. Who was the lead singer with the Tourists that had a
top 5 hit single in 1979?

14. "The Young New Mexican Puppeteer" was a 1972
hit single for what singer?

15. Bobbie Gentry's "Ode to Billy Joe" was a hit single
in what year?

16. "Low" was a 1977 hit album for what
singer/songwriter?

17. "Rainbow Valley" was a hit single for what group in
1968?

18. Who was lead singer with Led Zeppelin?

19. What song from "The Beatles " [AKA 'The White
Album'] gave Marmalade a number 1 hit single in 1969?

20. Who was lead singer with Status Quo?

Quiz 15 Bonus Question:
What was the first 'Blues' song to top the UK singles chart?

QUIZ NUMBER 16

1. How many days a week did the Beatles sing about in a track from their 1964 "Beatles for Sale" album?

2. What famous Country singer recorded the album "Gentleman Jim " in 1964?

3. "Hey Girl Don't Bother Me" was a 1971 hit for what group that got its name for the headwear they wore while performing?

4. What instrument did Muff Winwood play in the Spencer Davis Group?

5. "Take Me to The - -" was a 1973 hit single for Paul Simon. What are the two missing words in the song's title?

6. What group - that were at one time called 'The Hawks' - recorded the hit album "Cahoots" in 1971?

7. From which classic hit do the following lyrics appear?
"She said you hurt her so
She almost lost her mind
But now she says she knows
You're not the hurtin' kind"?

8. "Let Your Love Flow" was a 1976 hit single for what American duo?

9. The Equals had one number 1 hit single. Can you

name the song?

10. Who was lead singer with The Jam?

11. Who was lead guitarist with Fleetwood Mac in the 1960s?

12. "Aladdin Sane" was a 1973 hit album for what singer/songwriter?

13. What group recorded the original version of "Twist and Shout"?

14. "The Only Living Boy In New York" by Simon and Garfunkel is on which of the duo's albums?

15. Who was lead guitarist in the group, Faces?

16. What singer had a top 5 hit single with the Bee Gees "To Love Somebody" in 1969?

17. What soul singer was 'Working in the Coalmine' in 1966?

18. Who was bass guitarist with The Jimi Hendrix Experience?

19. "Billion Dollar Babies" was a 1973 hit album by what singer/songwriter?

20. "Homburg" was a top 10 hit single in 1967 for what group?

Quiz 16 Bonus Question:
What is the EXACT title of The Bee Gees number 1 hit,
commonly known as " Massachusetts"?

QUIZ NUMBER 17

1. What singer/songwriter recorded the 1969 number 1 hit album "Nashville Skyline "?

2. Who sang lead vocals on the Beatles track "Rocky Racoon " from the White Album in 1968?

3. "You're Moving Out Today" was a 1977 hit single for what singer/songwriter?

4. "Cousin Norman" was a 1971 hit single for what mainly Scottish group?

5. Who wrote "Fire Brigade", a top 5 hit for the Move in 1968?

6. What song gave Amen Corner its only number 1 hit single?

7. From what classic number 1 hit single do the following lyrics appear?
"Well the band were playing and the booze began to flow
But the sound came over on the police car radio
Down at Precinct 49
Having a tear-gas of a time
Sergeant Baker got a call from the governor of the county jail"?

8. "The Man with a Child in His -"was a 1978 hit single for Kate Bush. What's the missing word in the title of the song?

9. Did "All or Nothing" by the Small Faces get to number 1 on the UK charts in 1966?

10. What group did Alan Price form after he left the Animals?

11. Who was the drummer with The Walker Brothers in the hit making years?

12. "I'm Still Waiting" was a number 1 hit single in 1971 for what American Superstar?

13. "Wish You Were Here" was a 1975 number 1 hit album for what group?

14. What was Gene Pitney's debut top ten hit single in the UK charts?

15. Who was the youngest member of the Wilson brothers in the Beach Boys?

16. "I'm a Writer Not a Fighter" was a 1973 hit album for what Irish born singer/songwriter?

17. "A Boy Named - " was a 1969 hit single for Johnnie Cash. What's the missing word in the title?

18. Who was the lead singer with Hot Chocolate?

19. "Baby Please Don't Go" was the debut hit single for what Northern Irish group?

20. Who wrote "Wichita Lineman", a hit single for Glen Campbell in 1968?

Bonus Question:
What is John Denver's only hit single in the UK charts?

QUIZ NUMBER 18

1. Who was the lead singer and chief songwriter with the American group, Bread?

2. What multi-instrumentalist had a number 1 hit album in 1973 with "Tubular Bells"?

3. What group had a 1966 hit single with "She's a Must to Avoid"?

4. Andrew Gold had a 1978 hit single with "Never Let Her Slip -". What's the missing word in the title?

5. "I Can See Clearly Now" was a 1972 top ten hit single for what singer?

6. In what classic song do the following lyrics appear?
"On a dark desert highway
Cool wind in my hair
Warm smell of colitas
Rising up through the air
Up ahead in the distance
I saw a shimmering light."?

7. What group's debut hit single in the UK was "New York Mining Disaster 1941"?

8. "King of the Road" was a 1965 number 1 hit single for what singer?

9. "Rubber Bullets" was a number 1 hit single for what group in 1973?

10. Who was bass guitarist with Queen in the hit making years?

11. What Tony Orlando and Dawn hit single kept "Brown Sugar" by the Rolling Stones off the number 1 spot in 1971?

12. What George Harrison song from The Beatles album "Rubber Soul" gave the Hollies a minor hit single in 1965/1966?

13. "All Day and All of the Night" was a hit single in 1964 for what group?

14. "Behind Closed Doors" was a 1974 hit single and album for what Country singer?

15. "A Question of Balance" was a 1970 number 1 hit album for what group?

16. Who was lead singer with The Strawbs?

17. Judith Durham was lead singer of what highly successful 1960's group?

18. "Gypsys Tramps And -" was a 1971 hit single for Cher. What's the missing word in the title?

19. Elton John's first number 1 hit single was a duet with Kiki Dee in 1976. What's the title of the song?

20. Who was lead singer with The Four Seasons?

Bonus Question:
Who was the first Egyptian born singer to top the UK singles chart?

QUIZ NUMBER 19

1. What American group recorded the 1971 album "L.A. Woman?

2. What was the Beatles fourth and last Christmas number 1 hit single?

3. "Silly Love," taken from the album, "Sheet Music," was a minor hit in 1974 for what group?

4. Who played bass guitar in the Tremeloes from 1966 to 1972?

5. Who was lead singer with T Rex?

6. What group had a 1969 number 1 hit single with "Something in the Air?

7. From what classic hit do the following lyrics appear?
"I love the colourful clothes she wears
And the way the sunlight plays upon her hair
I hear the sound of a gentle word
On the wind that lifts her perfume through the air".

8. What famous singer/songwriter had a 1973 hit single with "Take Me to The Mardi Gras"?

9. What was the name of Los Bravos' top ten hit single in 1966?

10. "Sheer Heart Attack" was a hit album by what group

in 1974?

11. What group's debut hit single was "Melting Pot" in 1969?

12. Who was the lead singer with The Boomtown Rats?

13. When Wayne Fontana began his solo career who took over lead vocals in the Mindbenders?

14. "Three Times a Lady" was a number 1 hit single for what group in 1978?

15. Who was the eldest of the Gibb brothers?

16. In what year did Rod Stewart and Ronnie Wood join the group, Faces?

17. What legendary singer had a number 1 hit single in 1966 with "Strangers in the Night "?

18. What song was Roxy Music's debut hit single in 1972?

19. In what part of London was The Kinks formed?

20. Who wrote "Blinded by the Light", a 1976 hit single for Manfred Mann's Earth Band?

Bonus Question:
Merle Kilgore and who wrote Ring of Fire", Johnnie Cash's 1963 hit single?

QUIZ NUMBER 20

1. What group's debut album was called "Outlandos D'Amour?

2. "Tossing and Turning" was a hit single for what group in 1965?

3. David Bowie had a hit single in 1977 with "Sound and -". What's the missing word in the title?

4. From what classic song do the following lyrics appear?
"Oh don't it hurt deep inside
To see someone do something to her
Oh don't it pain to see someone cry
How especially if that someone is her"?

5. Ian Hunter was lead singer with what group that had a hit with David Bowie's, "All the Young Dudes"?

6. Who wrote "If You Gotta Go, Go Now", a hit for Manfred Mann in 1965?

7. "Children of the Revolution" was a 1972 hit single for what group?

8. "And Then There Were Three" was a hit album for what group in 1978?

9. What classic Beatles hit replaced "Little Red Rooster" by the Rolling Stones at the top of the singles charts in

December 1964?

10. "You Make Me Feel Like -" was a hit single for Leo Sayer in 1976. Can you complete the title of the song?

11. "Spirits Having Flown " was a hit album for what group in 1979?

12. "Sweets for my Sweet" was a number 1 hit single in 1963 for what Liverpool group?

13. "Here Comes My Baby" was a 1967 hit single for what group?

14. "No Regrets" was a comeback hit single in 1976 for what trio?

15. "Loves Really Hurts Without You" was a 1976 hit single for what singer?

16. Who was bass guitarist with the Small Faces? He wrote many of the group's hits with Steve Marriott

17. Who wrote "Step Inside Love " for Cilla Black. A hit for her in 1968 and used as the theme song for her tv series "Cilla"?

18. What song was Abba's debut hit single in 1974?

19. What singer had a number 1 hit single in 1972 with "Puppy Love"?

20. Who wrote "Out of Time", a number 1 hit single for Chris Farlowe in 1966?

Bonus Question:
What was Paul Jones' debut hit single after leaving Manfred Mann in 1966?

QUIZ NUMBER 21

1. "Storm in a - " was a 1972 hit single for the Fortunes. What's the missing word in the song's title?

2. From what classic hit do the following lyrics appear?
"Old woman, old woman, don't treat me so mean
You're the meanest old woman that I've ever seen
I guess if you said so
I'll have to pack my things and go (that's right)?"

3. "Comfortably Numb" by Pink Floyd came from which album?

4. Who had the original hit of "Three Steps to Heaven" in 1960?

5. "Cool for Cats" was a 1979 hit single for what group?

6. What singer/songwriter recorded the 1978 album "Whatever Happened to Benny Santini"?

7. Who was the lead singer with Dawn?

8. In what year did the Searchers have the number 1 hit "Don't Throw Your Love Away"?

9. Ron and Russell Mael were members of what 1970s group?

10. Who produced "I Can't Explain", the debut top ten hit single for The Who in 1965?

11. What group had the 1975 hit single/album with "One of These Nights?"

12. What was The Supremes debut hit single in the U.K. charts?

13. "Face the Music" was a 1975 album by what group?

14. The Overlanders had a 1966 number 1 hit single with what Beatles song?

15. "The Killing of Georgie Part I and II" was a 1976 hit single for what singer/songwriter?

16. What was the Troggs debut hit single?

17. "Don't Shoot Me, I'm Only the Piano Player" was a 1973 hit album for what singer/songwriter?

18. Who was the drummer with the Small Faces in the 1960s?

19. Who was lead singer with Sweet?

20. Who had a number 1 hit single in 1967 with "Let the Heartaches Begin"?

Bonus Question
Who played drums on the Marvelettes 1961 Motown single "Please Mister Postman"?

QUIZ NUMBER 22

1. "Songs in the Key Of Life" is a 1976 album by what singer/songwriter?

2. "Frozen Orange Juice" was a 1969 summer hit for what singer that was a follow-up to his number 1 hit single in the Spring of that year?

3. "Tumbleweed Connection" was a top ten hit album for what singer/songwriter in 1970?

4. *From what classic hit do the following lyrics appear?*
"Every day's an endless stream
Of cigarettes and magazines
And each town looks the same to me
The movies and the factories"?

5. Who was lead singer with Slade?

6. Which Beatles album was released on the 26th. September 1969?

7. Who was the lead singer with The Four Seasons?

8. "I Can't Let Maggie Go "was a top ten hit in 1968 for what group?

9. Who was lead singer with Mungo Jerry?

10. The Love Affair had a number 1 hit single with "Everlasting Love" in January 1968, but what group was first offered the song and turned it down?

11. Richard Tandy was keyboardist with what famous group in the 1970s?

12. Clive Powell had three number 1 hit singles in the 1960s under what name?

13. The old Everly Brothers song, "All I Have to Do Is Dream" was covered by what duo who had a hit with it in 1969/1970?

14. "Planet Waves" was a 1974 top ten album for what legendary singer/songwriter?

15. "Little Red Rooster" was a number 1 hit single for what group in December 1964?

16. "Can't Get by Without You" was a top five hit single for what group in 1976?

17. From what classic hit do the following lyrics appear?
"It wasn't me that started
That old crazy Asian war
But I was proud to go
And do my patriotic chore"?

18. "Armed Forces " was a 1979 hit album by what singer/songwriter?

19. In what year did "Concrete and Clay" by Unit Four Plus Two top the charts?

20. What song was The Spencer Davis Group's first number 1 hit single?

Bonus Question:
Which single was the first simultaneously transatlantic number 1 hit for the Beatles?

QUIZ NUMBER 23

1. Born To Run" was a 1975 hit single and album for what singer/songwriter?

2. Who wrote "Going' Back", a hit for Dusty Springfield in 1966?

3. Kenny Rogers, Kim Carnes, Gene Clark, and Barry McGuire were members of what 1960s folk group?

4. From what classic hit do the following lyrics appear?
" Dear Sir or Madam will you read my book?
It took me years to write, will you look"?

5. Is the Cat Stevens' song "Father and Son" track autobiographical?

6. Who was lead singer with Procol Harum?

7. What group recorded the 1972 album "Exile on Main Street"?

8. Who took Tony Jackson's place in the Searchers in 1964?

9. Terry Uttley was the bass player with what group in the 1970s?

10. "Last Night in Soho" was a 1968 hit single for what group?

11. "So You Win Again" was a number 1 hit single for what group in 1977?

12. "Dancing on a Saturday - " was a hit single for Barry Blue in 1973. What's the missing word in the title of the song?

13. "Bernadette " was a 1967 hit single for what Motown group?

14. "Wish You Were Here" was a 1975 hit album for what group?

15. "Look Through Any Window" was a 1965 hit single for the Hollies. Who wrote the song?

16. From what famous hit do the following lyrics appear?
"Is This the Real Life?
Is This Just Fantasty?
Caught In a Landslide
No Escape From reality"?

17. Who took over as lead singer with Genesis after Peter Gabriel left the group?

18. "Long Tall Glasses " was a 1974 hit single for what singer?

19. Who was "Saved by The Bell" in 1969?

20. Which member of the Moody Blues had a solo hit single with "Forever Autumn" in 1978?

Quiz 23 Bonus Question:
Deniece Williams had a number 1 hit single in 1977 with the song "Free" which kept Stevie Wonder's "Sir Duke" off the top spot. Coincidentally Williams sang in Stevie's backing group in the early 1970s. What was the name of the group?

QUIZ NUMBER 24

1. "It's All Over Now" was a number 1 hit single for what group in 1964?

2. From what chart topper of the 1970s do the following lyrics appear?
"Now, I understand what you tried to say to me
And how you suffered for your sanity
And how you tried to set them free
They would not listen, they did not know how
Perhaps they'll listen now"?

3. "What's New Pussycat" was a top twenty single for Tom Jones in 1965. Who wrote the song?

4. "Rocky Mountain High" was a 1973 hit album for what singer?

5. What group had the 1968 hit called "High in the Sky?

6. What group had a 1975 hit with the old Buddy Holly song "Heartbeat"?

7. Love Sculpture had a 1969 top ten hit with what instrumental?

8. "Calling Occupants of Interplanetary -" was a 1977 hit for the Carpenters. What is the missing word in the title of the song?

9. There were four members of Creedence Clearwater Revival...John Fogerty, Stu Cook, Doug Clifford were three members. Who was the fourth?

10. What duo had a top 20 hit single in 1966 with "(You're My) Soul and Inspiration"?

11. "Move on Up" was a top 20 hit for what soul singer in 1971?

12. "Frozen Orange Juice" was a 1969 hit for what singer?

13. "Another Saturday Night" was a hit single for Cat Stevens in 1974, but who wrote the song and *had a hit with it in 1963?*

14. What group turned down the chance to release "How Do You Do It "as a single? Gerry and the Pacemakers had no such qualms and had a number 1 hit with the song in 1963?

15. "Stand Up" was a hit album in 1969 for what group whose leader sang and played flute?

16. The Beatles "Got to Get You into My Life" was a top 20 hit for what group in 1966?

17. Who was the lead singer with Blondie?

18. "Excerpt from A Teenage Opera " was a 1967 hit single for what singer?

19. What legendary soul singer released the album "Talking Book" in 1972?

20. From what number one 1965 hit single do the following lyrics appear?
"All around
I see the purple shades of evening
And on the ground
The shadows fall and once again you're in my arms
So tenderly"?

Bonus Question:
Who played the bass intro to Carly Simon's 1973 hit, "You're So Vain"?

QUIZ NUMBER 25

1. "How Long" was a 1974 hit single for what group whose lead singer was Paul Carrick?

2. "Blue" was a 1971 hit album for what folk singer/songwriter?

3. Who was lead guitarist with the Small Faces?

4. "I'm Stone in Love with You" was a 1972 hit for what American group?

5. In what classic hit do the following lyrics appear?
"I see the girls walk by
Dressed in their summer clothes
I have to turn my head
Until my darkness goes"?

6. What Motown group had a 1967 hit with the single, "Bernadette"?

7. "Good Morning - " was a 1977 hit for 10cc. What's the missing word in the title?

8. Who sang lead vocals on the Beatles 1969 single, "Come Together"?

9. "Up the Junction" was a 1979 hit for what group?

10. What group had the number 1 hit album, "On the Threshold of a Dream" in 1969?

11. "Brand New Key" was a 1972 hit single for what singer/songwriter?

12. Yesterday's Has Gone" was a top ten hit single in the summer of 1968 for what group?

13. In what classic single do the following lyrics appear?
"I recall the yellow cotton dress
Foaming like a wave
On the ground around your knees
The birds, like tender babies in your hands
And the old men playing checkers by the trees"?

14. Who was lead singer with Curved Air?

15. Who was the only non-Beatle to receive a credit on a Beatles single?

16. "Have You Seen Her?" was a 1972 hit for what group?

17. "Kissing in the Back Row - - -" was a 1974 hit by the Drifters. What are the three missing words in the title?

18. "Pamela, Pamela " was a 1966 hit for what singer?

19. "Telephone Line" was a hit single for what group in 1977?

20. Who was lead single with the Yardbirds?

Bonus Question:
Mick Avory was the Kinks drummer in the hit making years. Even so, he didn't play drums in the recording of the singles "You Really Got Me" "All Day and All of the Night" and "Tired of Waiting for You". Can you name the session drummer who played on these three recordings?

QUIZ NUMBER 26

1. "A Nod's as Good as A Wink....To a Blind Horse" was a number 2 hit album in 1971 for what group?

2. What famous singer had a number 1 hit single with "Crying in the Chapel " in 1965?

3. Who had a 1975 hit single in the UK and US charts with "Eighteen with a Bullet?

4. Who was the first ex-Beatle to have a number 1 hit single in the UK?

5. "With a Girl Like You" was a 1966 number 1 hit single for what group?

6. From what classic hit do the following lyrics appear?
" Ah wouldn't it be nice
To get on with me neighbours
But they make it very clear
They've got no room for ravers"?

7. "Regatta De Blanc" was a number 1 hit album in 1979 for what group?

8. "Ruby Don't Take Your Love to Town" was a number 2 hit single for what singer, and his group, in 1969/1970?

9. How did the group 'McGuinness Flint ' get its name?

10. Who sang lead vocals on the Monkees 1967 hit

"Alternate Title"?

11. Was Paul Jones lead singer with Manfred Mann on its 1968 number 1 hit "Mighty Quinn"?

12. "Walls and Bridges " was a 1974 hit album for what singer/Songwriter?

13. "John Barleycorn Must Die" was a hit album in 1970 for what group?

14. Complete the title of Bob Dylan's 1965 hit single "Subterranean Homesick -"?

15. The Tremeloes had a 1969 number 2 hit single with "(Call Me) - -". Can You complete the title?

16. The UK's Eurovision entry in 1975 was "Let Me Be the One". What group came second in the contest with the song?

17. "How Dare You" was a 1976 hit album for what group?

18. What was the Christmas number 1 hit single in the charts in 1966?

19. What band had a top 5 hit single in 1977 with "2.4.6.8. Motorway"?

20. What was Blue Mink's debut hit single in 1969?

11. David McWilliams released "The Days Of - - " in 1967. Can you complete the song's title?

12. "Don't it Make My Brown Eyes Blue" was a 1978 hit for what Country singer?

13. "Long Live Love" was a 1965 number 1 hit single for what singer?

14. Nilsson had the best-selling single in 1972 with what song?

15. Who was the original keyboardist with the Animals?

16. What was Bob Marley's backing group called?

17. In what year did "California Girls" first enter the UK charts....1965 or 1966?

18. Who became lead singer with the Moody Blues after Denny Laine left the group?

19. In what country was folk singer, Gordon Lightfoot born?

20. Who sang lead vocals on the Eagles "Hotel California"?

Bonus Question:
When Dusty Springfield went on tour in the 1960s, what was the name of the backing band she used?

QUIZ NUMBER 28

1. "World Without Love" was a number 1 hit single for what duo in 1964?

2. Who was the lead singer with The Seekers?

3. In what year did Brian Jones Die?

4. Who were "Terry and Julie" rumoured to be in the Kinks hit, "Waterloo Sunset"?

5. What is Eric Clapton's nickname?

6. In what year was "Pet Sounds" by The Beachboys released?

7. Who was the lead singer with the Belfast group Them?

8. The Beatles recorded two albums in 1964. One was "A Hard Day's Night." Can you name the second album?

9. Who was voted "The Face of 1968"?

10. Were Paul and Barry Ryan twins?

11. Who was the lead singer with The Walker Brothers?

12. Who was the drummer in 10cc?

13. "I'd Rather Go Blind" was a hit single for Chicken

Shack in 1969. Who was the group's lead singer?

14. The Kinks had one number 1 hit single in 1966. Can you name it?

15. "Tears on My Pillow" was a number 1 hit single for what singer"?

16. "Yester-Me, Yester-You, Yesterday" was a top 10 hit single for who in 1968?

17. "Where Are You Now (My Love)" was a number 1 hit single for what singer in 1965?

18. "Are You Ready to Rock" was a 1975 hit single for what group?

19. From what number 1 hit single do the following lyrics appear?
"Father McKenzie
writing the words of a sermon that no one will hear
No one comes near
Look at him working."

20. "They Shoot Horses, Don't They" was a 1977 hit single for what group?

Bonus Question
What singer's first seven singles reached the top 10; a feat first achieved in 1961 by the singer's manager?

QUIZ NUMBER 29

1. The Bay City Rollers had a number 1 hit single in 1975 with a song first made famous by The Four Seasons. Can you name the song?

2. "The First Time Ever I Saw Your Face" was a 1972 hit single for what singer?

3. "Junior's Farm" was a top 30 hit single in 1974 for what act?

4. Did Barry White have more than one number 1 hit singles?

5. Who was the lead singer with Pilot?

6. "Wichita Lineman" was a hit single for Glen Campbell. Who wrote the song?

7. Mason Williams had a 1968 top ten instrumental hit. Can You name the hit?

8. "Four-Way Street" was a 1971 hit album for what supergroup?

9. Eve Graham and Lynn Paul were lead singers with what group?

10. "Harper Valley PTA" was a 1968 hit single by what singer?

11. In what city was Jeff Lynne born?

12. "At Seventeen" was a 1975 recording by what American singer/songwriter?

13. Tony Jackson was a member of a Liverpool group before being replaced in 1964. Can you name the group?

14. The four members of the Mamas and Papas were, John and Michelle Phillips, Cass Elliott. Who was the fourth member?

15. "The Carnival is Over" was a number 1 hit in 1965 by what group?

16. "Pool Hall Richard" was a hit single for what group in 1973?

17. Eddie Kendricks was one of several singers in what famous Motown group from the early 1960's to 1971?

18. "It's Impossible" was a 1971 hit single for what singer?

19. What is Elton John's birth name?

20. In what city was Rod Stewart born?

Bonus Question
Who sang lead vocals on Chicago's 1976 number 1 hit single, "If You Leave Me Now"?

QUIZ NUMBER 30

1. Did the Hollies have a number 1 hit single in the 1970's?

2. "Himself" is a 1971 album by what singer/songwriter?

3. "Don't Let Me Be -" was a hit for the Animals in 1965. What's the missing word in the title?

4. What singer had a 1974 hit with "Hang on in There Baby"?

5. "Natural Born Boogie" was a 1969 top ten hit for what group?

6. Only two acts have achieved the feat of getting three albums to number 1 in the album charts in one year in either the 1960s or 1970s. The first act is The Beatles in 1965. What is the second act?

7. Who wrote "Rocking all Over the World", a 1977 top 3 hit single for Status Quo?

8. From which number 2 hit single in 1971 do the following lyrics appear?
"The tiger's free, the kangaroo
It's up to me and up to you.
What we see is what we choose
What we keep or what we lose forever"

9. Matt Monroe had a top ten hit single in 1965 with a Beatles song. Which song?

10. "Hold Me Close" was a number 1 hit single in 1975 for what singer?

11. What Motown star was too busy thinking about his baby in 1969?

12. What group had a hit in 1977 with "Car Wash"?

13. The song "Valleri" was a 1968 top twenty hit single for what group?

14. Who was lead singer with Harold Melvin and the Bluenotes?

15. What's was Pink Floyd's debut top twenty hit single?

16. Which group made the most appearances on 'Top of the Pops'?

17. What group were "Glad All Over" in 1964?

18. "Things" was a 1962 hit single for what American singer?

19. In what year did the TV pop programme "Ready, Steady, Go "begin broadcasting?

20. What was the Beach Boys follow-up single to "I Get Around"?

Quiz 30 Bonus question:
Mama Cass Elliott (1974) and Keith Moon (1978) both died in the same London apartment owned by what singer/songwriter?

QUIZ NUMBER 31
Hit singles of 1966

1. My Ship Is Coming In" was a hit single for what act?

2. "A Lover's Concerto" was a hit single for what American girl group?

3. Otis Redding had a hit single in this year that was more popular when The Temptations recorded it. Can you name the song?

4. "Spanish Flea" was a hit for what American group?

5. "Let's Hang On" was a top 10 hit single for what group?

6. The Beatles, "Michelle" was a number 1 hit single for what group?

7. "Till the End Of the –"was a top 10 single for the Kinks. Can you complete the title of the song?

8. "Second Hand Rose" was a top 20 hit single for what singer?

9. "Like a Baby" was a top 10 hit single for what singer?

10. "Pinkerton's Assorted Colours" had a top 10 hit with what song this year?

11. "Love's Just a Broken Heart" was a hit for what Liverpool born singer?

12. "Inside Looking Out" was a hit for what group?

13. Did "Barbara Ann" by the Beach Boys top the charts in 1966?

14. "Shapes of Things" was a top 10 hit for what group?

15. "Make the World Go Away" was a hit for what American Country singer?

16. Roy C had a top 10 hit single with what song?

17. "Hey Girl" was a top 10 hit for the Small Faces. Who wrote the song?

18. From what classic hit do the following lyrics appear?
"When she walks by, she brightens up the neighbourhood
Oh every guy would make her his
If he just could
If she just would."

19. Georgie Fame had a number 1 hit in the summer of this year. Can you name the song?

20. "Goin' Back" was a top 10 hit for Dusty Springfield. Who wrote the song?

Bonus Question
"Backstage" was a top 10 hit single for what singer?

QUIZ NUMBER 32
1960's Albums

1. What group recorded the album "If You Can Believe Your Eyes and Ears"? In 1966?

2. "Ramblin' Rose" was a 1962 album for what singer?

3. Bob Dylan had a hit album in 1965 with "Bringing It All Back – ". Can you complete the album's title?

4. "Out of our Heads" was a 1965 album by what group?

5. "I Just Wasn't Made for These Times" is a track off which 1966 album?

6. "The Soft Parade" is a 1969 album by what group?

7. What duo recorded the album "Bookends" in 1968?

8. "Cheap Thrills" is an album by what group?

9. What English group recorded the concept album "Tommy" in 1969?

10. "Bayou Country" is a 1969 album by what group?

11. What legendary singer recorded the album "Blue Hawaii"?

12. "Parsley, Sage, Rosemary and Thyme" is a 1966 album by what duo?

13. "At Folsom Prison" is a 1968 album by what singer?

14. Creedence Clearwater Revival had the 1969 hit album called "Green – ". Can you name the missing word in the album's title?

15. "Moondance" is a 1969 album by what singer/songwriter?

16. "Waiting For the Sun" is a 1968 album by what group"?

17. "Electric Ladyland" was a hit album for what group?

18. "Beggars Banquet "was a hit album in 1968 for what group?

19. The Beach Boys had a hit album in 1963 with the album "Little Deuce –". What's the missing word in the title?

20. "Days of Wine and Roses" was a hit album by what singer?

Bonus Question:
From what Bob Dylan album did the tracks "Sad Eyed Lady of the Lowlands" and "4th Time Around" Come off?

QUIZ NUMBER 33

1. What member of a leading 1960s group that never had a number 1 hit single in the UK produced a number 1 hit single for another group in 1969?

2. Who had a 1971 hit album called, "What's Going On"?

3. Bill Martin and who wrote the 1967 Eurovision winner, "Puppet on A String" by Sandie Shaw?

4. What group had a 1973 UK hit with, "Tie a Yellow Ribbon Round the Old Oak Tree"?

5. Who was the lead guitarist with The Kinks?

6. Johnny Bristol's 1974 smash hit was called, "Hang on in There -". What's the missing word from the title?

7. What Beatles album does, "You're Gonna Lose That Girl" appear?

8. "Living in the Material World" was a hit album in 1973 for what musician?

9. What group sang the original version of, "Silence is Golden"?

10. "God Save The Queen" was a UK hit in 1977 for what group?

11. In the 1960s and 1970s and beyond, who was the oldest member of the Rolling Stones?

12. "Moonshadow" is on which of Cat Stevens albums?

13. What girl group had a 1968 UK hit with, "Something Here in My Heart"?

14. What famous American group recorded the "Holland" album in 1973?

15. "The Price of Love" was a 1965 hit for what duo?

16. "Native New Yorker "was a top 10 hit for what group in 1978?

17. "The Next Time"/" Bachelor Boy" was a double (A) sided number 1 hit single for what singer in 1963?

18. "Please Mr Postman" was a 1975 number 2 hit for what duo?

19. "One and One is One" was a 1973 hit single by what group?

20. "Pyjamarama" was a top 10 hit single for what group in 1973?

Bonus Question:
In what venue did the Jimi Hendrix Experience play its debut gig in 1966?

QUIZ NUMBER 34

1. Who wrote, "Rose Garden", a hit for Lynn Anderson in 1971?

2. "Alfie" by Cilla Black was a hit single in what year?

3. Which ex member of Marmalade had a top twenty hit with "Sweet Illusion" in 1973?

4. Who wrote "Build Me Up Buttercup" for the Foundations?

5. "Children of the Revolution " was a 1972 number 2 UK hit single for what group?

6. What song is on the (B) side of the Beatles, "All You Need Is Love"?

7. Who was lead singer with the group Sweet?

8. "Wives and Lovers " was a hit for what singer in 1963?

9. What was 10cc's last album with the four original members?

10. What year was "Happy Together " by the Turtles a hit in the UK charts?

11. What duo wrote, "Tequila Sunrise", a hit for the Eagles in 1973?

12. What is the only George Harrison song to be issued as a Beatles single in the UK?

13. From which ELO album was "Rockaria" taken off and issued as a single?

14. What group had a 1964 UK hit single with, "Chapel of Love"?

15. "Back to the -" is a Wings album released in 1979. What's the missing word in the title?

16. "Mr Fantasty" was a 1967 hit album for what group?

17. "I Was Made to Love" was a top 10 single for what singer in 1967?

18. Art Garfunkel had a number 1 hit single in 1979 with what song?

19. Joe Cocker had a number 1 hit single in 1968 with what Beatles song?

20. "Yesterday Once More" was a top 5 hit single in 1973 for what duo?

Bonus Question:
What is the only hit single where the title of the song and name of the group are both palindromes?

QUIZ NUMBER 35

1. "Be Young, Be Foolish, Be Happy" was a UK number 32 hit for what group in 1970?

2. "Come and Stay with Me" was a UK top 5 hit for Marianne Faithfull in 1965. Who wrote the song?

3. "Making Plans For -----" was a UK hit for XTC in 1979. What word is missing from the title?

4. On what classic hit do these lyrics appear?
"So many days you passed me by. See the tear standing in my eye. You didn't stop to make me feel better, by leaving me a card or a letter".

5. What group had a 1975 hit single with, "Lyin' Eyes"?

6. Cat Stevens ' "Wild World" was on which of his albums

7. "Strange Brew" was a 1967 UK top twenty hit single for what group?

8. What singer/songwriter had a 1977 hit album called, "The Stranger"?

9. What famous singer/songwriter wrote, "I'll Be Your Baby Tonight"?

10. What British group released the album, "Venus and Mars" in 1975?

11. How many miles high were The Byrds in 1966?

12. What was Gilbert O'Sullivan's debut UK hit single in 1970?

13. What group had a 1967 UK hit with, "Itchycoo Park"?

14. "Love's in Need of Love Today" is the opening track on what Stevie Wonder album?

15. On what classic hit do the following lyrics appear?
"Need to hold you, once again, my love.
Feel your warm embrace, my love
Don't throw our love away. lease don't do me this way"?

16. "The Tra-La Days Are Over" was a hit album for what singer in 1973?   N. Sedaka

17. "Sunshine of Your Love" was a hit single for what group in 1968

18. The group Pussycat had a number 1 hit single in 1976. Can you name the song?

19. "Oh Well" gave what group a top 5 hit single in 1969?

20. What was the bestselling single in 1972?

Bonus Question:
 Who played Synthesiser on Marianne Faithfull's version of "The Ballad of Lucy Jordan" in 1979?

QUIZ NUMBER 36

1. What duo recorded the Jagger/Richards song, "Sittin' on A Fence" in 1966?

2. From what Wings album does the track, "Bluebird" appear?

3. What group had a 1965 UK hit with, "Here it Comes Again"?

4. "Coz I Luv You" was a 1971 number 1 UK hit for what group?

5. Who was Marmalade's lead guitarist in the '60s?

6. Johnny Nash had a 1975 UK hit with the single, "Tears on my -". What's the missing word in the title?

7. Who wrote the Move's 1968 hit, "Fire Brigade"?

8. Who was tired of being alone in the 1971 UK charts?

9. "A New World Record" is a 1976 album for what group?

10. What singer had the 1979 UK hit single with, "Oliver's Army"?

11. From which classic Kinks hit single do the following lyrics appear?
"I like my football on a Saturday

Roast beef on Sundays, all right. I go to Blackpool for my holidays
Sit in the open sunlight"?

12. "Parallel Lines " was a 1978 hit album for what group?

13. One of my all-time favourite albums is "Silk Degrees". What singer recorded this classic in 1976?

14. On what Beatles album does, "Honey Pie" appear?

15. Another lyric; what 1965 hit do these lyrics come from?
"I could see right out my window, walkin' down the street my girl, with another guy
his arm around her, like it used to be with me".

16. "Blockbuster" was a number 1 hit in 1973 for what group?

17. "Curly" was a hit single for what group in 1969?

18. "The Last Farewell" was a top 20 hit single for what singer in 1975?

19. Cat Stevens had a top ten hit single in 1967 with "I'm Gonna Get Me a –". What's the missing word in the title?

20. "When Will I See You Again" was a number 1 hit single for what group in 1974?

Quiz 36 Bonus Question:
The final track ("The Last Resort") of the Eagles "Hotel California" album, had to be re-recorded a number of times due to noise from the next studio by what band?

QUIZ NUMBER 37

1. Who was lead singer with Herman's Hermits?

2. What group had a 1968 UK hit with, "Last Night in Soho"?

3. What was Marc Bolan's birth name?

4. What was Amen Corner's debut hit single in the UK?

5. What was Georgie Fame's backing band called?

6. How many number 1 hit singles in the UK did the Tremeloes have in the 1960s?

7. Was Tom Fogerty lead vocalist with Creedence Clearwater Revival?

8. Who was the main songwriter with, The Mamas and The Papas?

9. In what year did the Bee Gees have its first UK hit?

10. Who had a 1961 UK hit single with, "Johnny Remember Me"?

11. What hit do the following lyrics appear in?
"Cleaned a lot of plates in Memphis
Pumped a lot of tane down in New Orleans
But I never saw the good side of the city
Until I hitched a ride on a riverboat queen"

12. What was Joe South's only top ten UK hit single in the 1960s?

13. Another lyric? What song do these lyrics come from?
" Dragging my soul to a beautiful land
Something has invaded my mind
Painting my sleep with a colour so bright
Changing the grey and changing the blue"

14. What duo wrote the above song?

15. What group has a 1968 UK hit single with, "Ain't Nothing but a Housepart# "?

16. "It's Only Rock and Roll" was a 1974 top ten for what group?

17. "Cold Turkey" was a hit single in 1969 for what group?

18. "I Only Have Eyes for You" was a number 1 for what singer in 1975?

19. Vikki Carr had a number 2 hit single in 1967 with what song?

20. What is the connection between Peter Sarstedt, and Eden Kane?

Quiz 37 Bonus Question:

Roger McGuinn - before he formed the Byrds - was a member of what famous singer's band in the early 1960s?

QUIZ NUMBER 38

1. Who produced "Those Were the Days" the number 1 hit for Mary Hopkin in 1968?

2. "London Calling" was a hit album in 1979 for what group?

3. "Listen to What the Man Said" was a hit single in 1975 for what act?

4. "Deja Vu" was a hit album for what group in 1970?

5. Who sang lead vocals on the Beach Boys 1965 hit single "Help Me Rhonda?"

6. "Juliet" was a 1964 number 1 hit single for what group?

7. Who was the drummer with The Band?

8. What song was the Kinks first number 1 hit single in 1964?

9. "Pearl's A Singer" was a 1977 for what singer?

10. "Suddenly You Love Me" was a 1968 hit for what group?

11. "Back to Front" was a 1972 hit album for what singer/songwriter?

12. Long John Baldry had one number 1 hit single in our

timeframe. Can you name it?

13. "Mercy Mercy Me" was a hit single for Marvin Gaye in 1971. What album did the song come off?

14. Who sang lead vocals on "Loving Things," the debut hit for The Marmalade in 1968?

15. From what famous 1979 hit single do the following lyrics appear?
"Hong Kong is up for grabs
London is full of Arabs
We could be in Palestine
Overrun by the Chinese line
With the boys from the Mersey and the Thames and the Tyne"?

16. What singer had a 1969 hit single with "Dizzy?"

17. "Seasons in the Sun" was a 1974 number 1 hit single for what singer?

18. Which two Beatles didn't play on the group's 1969 number 1 hit, "The Ballad of John and Yoko"?

19. "Le Freak" was a 1978 hit single for what group?

20. The 1965 PJ Proby hit single, "Maria" comes from which famous musical?

Bonus Question:
The (B) side of the Applejack's 1964 hit "Tell Me When" was a song called "Baby Jane" written by Pete

Dello and Ray Cane. Four years later, the duo formed a group that had a top ten hit single. Can you name the group and the hit?

QUIZ NUMBER 39

1. "What's Going On" was a 1971 album by which Motown singer/songwriter?

2. What group had a 1968 hit single called, "Captain of Your Ship"?

3. What singer had a top ten hit single with "I Can See Clearly Now" in 1972?

4. "Honky Chateau" was a top 5 hit album in 1972 for what singer/songwriter?

5. Which Irish trio had a hit single with Paul Simon's "The Sound of Silence" in 1966?

6. "Moonlighting" was a top 3 hit single for who in 1975?

7. From what classic hit do the following lyrics appear?
"Cool town, evening in the city
Dressed so fine and lookin' so pretty
Cool cat lookin' for a kitty
Gonna look in every corner of the city"?

8. In what year did "Dancing Queen" by Abba top the charts?

9. "Poor Man's Son" was a 1965 hit single for what group?

10. What singer had a 1973 hit single with Dylan's "A Hard Rain's A-Gonna Fall"?

11. In what year was "Rumours" by Fleetwood Mac released?

12. "Sleepy Joe" was a 1968 hit single for what group?

13. "Can't Get by Without You" was a top 5 hit single for what group in 1976?

14. What was the Move's only number 1 hit single?

15. "Under the Moon of Love " was a number 1 hit single for what group in 1976?

16. What group had a 1967 hit single with "The Happening"?

17. Trini Lopez had a 1963 hit with the single "If I Had a – ". What's the missing word in the title?

18. Who sang lead vocals on the Eagles track "Desperado"?

19. "Viva Bobby Joe" was a 1969 hit single for what group?

20. What was Leo Sayer's debut top ten single?

Bonus Question:
What singer/songwriter transformed his life after almost drowning off the coast of Malibu in 1976?

QUIZ NUMBER 40

1. Julie Driscoll and the Brian Auger Trinity had a 1968 hit single with what Bob Dylan song?

2. "Run to Me" was a 1972 hit single for what group?

3. What famous blues group released the album, "Then Play On" in 1969?

4. What singer/songwriter had a hit album called "52nd Street" in 1978?

5. From what famous hit do the following lyrics appear?
*"Baby, there's an enormous crowd of people
And they're all after my blood
I wish maybe they'd tear down the walls of this theatre
And let me out, let me out"*

6. Who had a top twenty hit single with "Come on Home" in 1966?

7. What legendary singer/songwriter had a hit single in 1974 with "Living for The City"?

8. Who sang lead vocal on the Moody Blues 1965 number 1 single "Go Now"?

9. Complete the title of this 1975 hit by the Stylistics "I Can't Give You Anything - - -"

10. "My name is Jack" was a hit single for what group in 1968?

11. "Mud Slide Slim and the Blue Horizon" was an album for what singer in 1971?

12. Who wrote "All the Young Dudes", a hit single for Mott the Hoople in 1972?

13. Complete the title, "Move Over -" which was a hit for Doris Day on 1964

14. Who had a hit with "Rose Garden" in 1971?

15. What was the debut hit single for the Who?

16. "Sunday Girl" was a number 1 hit single for what group?

17. "Red Rose Speedway" was a 1973 hit album for what act?

18. "For Once In My –"was a 1969 hit single for Stevie Wonder. What's the missing word in the song's title?

19. "Milk and Alcohol" was a hit single for what group in 1979?

20. "Even the Bad Times Are Good" was a 1967 hit single for what popular group?

Bonus Question:
Which member of Chicago accidently fatally shot himself in January 1978?

QUIZ NUMBER 41

1. What singer had a top 5 hit album in 1972 with "Portrait of Donny"?

2. Who was the "McGuire" mentioned in the Mamas and the Papas 1967 hit, "Creeque Alley"?

3. In what classic song do the following lyrics appear?
"Is there someone you know
Your loving them so
But taking them all for granted?
You may lose them one day
Someone takes them away
And they don't hear the words you long to say"?

4. What group had a number 1 hit single in 1978 with "Rat Trap"?

5. Joe Cocker had a hit single in 1969 with "Delta Lady". Who was the eponymous lady in the song?

6. Who was/is the drummer with Queen?

7. What British group had a 1966 album called "A Quick One"?

8. What American group had a hit single in 1978 with "Picture This"?

9. Who was lead singer and flautist with JethroTull?

10. "Did You Ever? "was a 1971 hit for which duo?

11. Was "Waterloo Sunset" by the Kinks a number 1 hit single in the UK in 1967?

12. The classic Motown song "This Old Heart of Mine" was a top 5 hit in 1975 for what singer?

13. "Hurdy Gurdy Man" was a hit single in 1968 for what singer/songwriter?

14. In what classic song do the following lyrics appear?
" Wanna play cricket on the green
Ride my bike across the street
Cut myself and see my blood
Wanna come home all covered in mud"

15. What folk singer had a 1971 hit single with "The Night They Drove Old Dixie Down"?

16. What Country singer had a posthumous number 1 single with "Distant Drums in 1966?

17. "Streets of London" was a number 2 hit single for what folk singer in 1975?

18. Gilbert O'Sullivan had a number 1 hit single in 1973 with what song?

19. Was "Lady Madonna" by the Beatles number 1 in 1968 or 1969?

20. Roxy Music had a number 2 hit single with "Dance —"in 1979. What's the missing word in the song's title?

Bonus Question:
Carl Wilson of the Beach Boys was taught how to play guitar in the early 1960s by someone who would have success as a singer as part of a trio in the mid-sixties. Can you name him?

QUIZ NUMBER 42

1. Who produced "Tobacco Road" for the Nashville Teens?

2. What singer had a UK 1964 hit called, "Boys Cry"?

3. What group had a UK hit in 1964 with, He's in Town"?

4. In what song do these lyrics appear?
"It's a thousand pages, give or take a few
I'll be writing more in a week or two"

5. What group had a UK hit in 1968 with, "Ice in the Sun"?

6. Chas Chandler - bassist with The Animals - managed what act from 1967 to the end of the decade?

7. What singer had a UK 1968 hit with, "If I Only Had Time "?

8. What was on Paul McCartney's knee when he was travelling "Back in the USSR"?

9. Who was the drummer in the Spencer Davis Group?

10. Here's another lyric, name the song.
"The room was humming harder
As the ceiling flew away
When we called out for another drink

The waiter brought a tray"

11. From which Beatles album does the track, "Baby's in Black" appear?

12. Who had a 1966 UK hit with, "Bang Bang"?

13. What French title did Stevie Wonder have in his hit in 1969?

14. Who was lead guitarist with the Equals?

15. The supergroup Cream consisted of Eric Clapton, Jack Bruce, and who else?

16. In what year did Elvis Presley die?

17. "Lonely Boy" was a top 20 hit single by what singer in 1977?

18. "Squeeze Box" was a 1976 hit single by what group?

19. "Every Picture Tells a Story "was a 1971 number 1 hit album for what singer/songwriter?

20. Who was lead singer with The Police?

Bonus Question:
Actor Will Farrell's father, Roy Lee Ferrell played keyboards and saxophone for a well-known act for many years. What act?

QUIZ NUMBER 43

1. Who was the lead singer with Queen?

2. Who was the lead singer with the Merseybeats?

3. "I'll Never Get Over You" was a 1963 UK hit for what singer and his group? ▪

4. From what classic song do these lyrics come from?
"I can tell the way you hang your head
You're without love and now you're afraid
And through your tears you look around
But there's no peace of mind to be found"?

5. "Here It Comes Again" is a 1965 UK top ten hit single for what group?

6. What singer sang the soundtrack to the 1967 Bond movie, "You Only Live Twice"?

7. Who was lead guitarist with The Hollies through the 1960s and beyond?

8. Who wrote the song, ""Suite: Judy Blue Eyes" a track by Crosby, Stills, and Nash on their eponymous 1969 album?

9. In what year was "Darlin' "by the Beach Boys a hit single in the UK charts?

10. Who was lead singer with the Yardbirds until its break-up in 1968?

11. Billy Fury was only halfway to where in his UK hit of 1961?

12. What is Elvis Presley's last number 1 hit in the UK in the 1960s?

13. In which classic song do these lyrics appear?
"He flits from shop to shop just like a butterfly
In matters of the cloth, he is as fickle as can be"?

14. "Breaking Up is Hard to Do" was a UK hit single by what singer in 1962?

15. Who began playing bass guitar in Manfred Mann before switching to lead guitar halfway through the 60s?

16. Who was the drummer with The Move in the hit making years of the 1960s and went on to be the drummer with ELO?

17. "I Can't Control Myself" was a hit single for what group in 1966?

18. How many number 1hit singles did Tom Jones have in the 1960's?

19. "Whatever You Want" was a 1979 top 10 single by what group?

20. "Walk Like a Man" was a top twenty single in 1963 for what group?

Bonus Question:

What's the connection between, Dave Berry's, "The Crying Game", PJ Proby's, "Hold Me", Gerry and The Pacemakers, "Ferry Cross The Mersey", Cilla Black's, "Anyone Who Had A Heart", Donovan's ,"Catch The Wind", and Jane Birkin and Serge Gainsbourg's (Je T'aime)?

QUIZ NUMBER 44

1. "Some Girls " was a hit album for what group in 1978?

2. "The Wind Cries Mary" was a top 10 single for what group in 1967?

3. Who was lead singer with the group Smokie in the hit making years?

4. Mike D'Abo's first hit single with Manfred Mann was with what Bob Dylan written song?

5. "48 Crash" was a 1973 top 3 hit single for what American singer?

6. "Jennifer Juniper" and "Jennifer Eccles " were both on the U.K. singles chart simultaneously in 1968. Which song was a hit for the Hollies?

7. "Turnstiles" was an album in 1974 for what American singer/songwriter?

8. From what classic 1964 hit single do the following lyrics appear?
"I guess I'll go on home, it's late
There'll be tomorrow night, but wait
What do I see?
Is she walkin' back to me?
Yeah, she's walkin' back to me."

9. "Don't Cry For Me Argentina" was a top 10 instrumental single - of the hit song from "Evita" - by what veteran group in 1979?

10. "Don't Forget To - " was a top 10 hit single in 1969 by the Bee Gees. What's the missing word in the title?

11. "Cool for Cats" was a hit single in 1979 for what group?

12. From what musical did "Good Morning Starshine " by Oliver come from?

13. "Isn't She Lovely", a hit single in 1977 for David Parton came from which Stevie Wonder album?

14. The Turtles had three top 20 hit singles in the UK chart between 1967 and 1968. What was the group's third and final hit?

15. Which future disco diva sang backing vocals on Three Dog Night's "Mama Told Me Not to Come" in 1970?

16. "Heart Full Of Soul" by the Yardbirds was kept off the number 1 spot in the singles charts in 1965 by what Bob Dylan song?

17. "You're More Than a Number in my - - -" was a top 10 hit single by the Drifters in 1977. Can you fill in the three missing words in the song's title?

18. Felix Cavaliere and Eddie Brigati were both members and songwriters with what American group?

19. Who was the drummer in the rock group, Queen throughout the 1970's and beyond?

20. "Don't Let It Die" by Hurricane Smith reached number 2 in the singles chart in 1971. What was Smith's real forename?

Bonus Question:
"Hideaway" was a 1966 hit single for what prolific hit making group?

QUIZ NUMBER 45

1. What singer/songwriter recorded the 1965 hit album, "Highway 61 Revisited?"

2. "Pearl's a Singer" was a top ten hit single for what female singer in 1977?

3. What song was Status Quo's debut hit single?

4. "Make Me Smile (Come Up and See Me")" was a number 1 hit single in 1975 for what act?

5. From what classic song - that was a hit in 1967 and again in 1973 - do the following lyrics appear?
"Gazing at people
Some hand in hand
Just what I'm going through
They can't understand
Some try to tell me
Thoughts they cannot defend
Just what you want to be
You will be in the end."

6. "Take Me To the - -" was a top ten hit single in 1973 for Paul Simon. Can you name the two missing words in the song's title?

7. The Bee Gees, "To Love Somebody " was a 1969 top five hit single for what singer?

8. "Hanging on the Telephone" was a top 5 hit single for what group in 1978?

9. How many number 1 hit singles did the Hollies have in the 1960's?

10. "Aqualung" and "Thick as a Brick" were hit albums for what group?

11. Who was the main songwriter in the group, The Mamas, and Papas?

12. "Lady Rose" was a top 5 hit single for what group in 1971?

13. Who was lead singer with Marmalade from 1966 to 1974?

14. "Angel"/What Made Milwaukee Famous " was a double A sided hit single for what singer in 1972?

15. "Going Up the - " was a hit single for Canned Heat in 1969. What's the missing word in the title?

16. "All the Young Dudes" was a hit single for Mott the Hoople in 1972. Who wrote the song?

17. How many top 20 hit singles did the Lemon Pipers have in the 1960's?

18. Billy Joel was in the singles chart at number 14 on the 9th.February 1979 with "My Life". One place above this was another Joel song recorded by Barry White. Can you name the song?

19. Was the Supremes debut hit single; "Baby Love" or "Where Did Our Love Go."?

20. "Howzat" was a top 4 hit single in 1976 for what Australian group?

Bonus Question
What punk/new wave act was the first to have a number 1 hit single?

QUIZ NUMBER 46
What Year Round

1. In what year did "She Loves You" by the Beatles top the charts?

2. "Kites" by Simon Dupree and the Big Sound was a hit in what year?

3. "I Can't Explain "by The Who was a hit in what year?

4. In what year did "If You Leave Me Now" by Chicago top the charts?

5. "Making Plans for Nigel" was a hit for XTC in what year?

6. "Out of the Blue" was a hit album for ELO in what year?

7. Dave Berry had a hit with the song "The Crying Game" in what year?

8. The Merseys had a hit with "Sorrow" in what year?

9. "Malt and Barley Blues" was a hit for McGuinness Flint in what year?

10. In what year did Lindsfarne have a hit with "Meet Me on the Corner"?

My Heart"?

11. "Big Yellow Taxi" was a 1970 hit single for what singer/songwriter?

12. Aretha Franklin had a 1968 hit single with a Burt Bacharach/Hal David song. Can you name it?

13. "You're So Vain" was a 1972/1973 hit for what singer/songwriter?

14. There were two female members of Fleetwood Mac. One was the late Christine McVie. Who was the other?

15. "I Feel Love" was a 1977 hit single for what Disco Diva?

16. "Tapestry" was a massive hit album for what singer/songwriter?

17. "The Way We Were" was a 1973 hit single and album for what singer?

18. What legendary Motown singer had a number 1 hit single in 1971 with, "I'm Still Waiting"?

19. "Devil Gate Drive" was a 1974 number 1 hit single for who?

20. "Terry" was a 1964 hit single for who?

Quiz 47 Bonus Question:
Anni-Frid Lyngstad was a member of what chart-topping group?

QUIZ NUMBER 48

1. "Hot Love" was a 1971 number 1 hit single for what group?

2. What were the forenames of The Everly Brothers?

3. Who was the drummer with the Young Rascals/Rascals in the 1960's?

4. Who were the two female singers with the New Seekers"?

5. The track "Harmony" came from which Elton John Album?

6. "No Regrets" was a hit single in 1975 for what group?

7. How did the singer John Denver die?

8. "All Things Must Pass" was a 1971 hit album for which ex-Beatle?

9. "Miss You Nights" was a 1976 hit single for what singer?

10. Which Monkee sang lead vocals on "Daydream Believer"?

11. Who was lead singer with the group, XTC?

12. "Behind Closed Doors" was a hit single in 1973 for what singer?

13. "Old Siam Sir" was a track on which Wings album?

14. Who was the bassist in The Small Faces?

15. "Alone again, Or" was a 1967 single by what group?

16. From what famous number 1 hit single do the following lyrics appear?
"Heathcliff, it's me, I'm Cathy
I've come home, I'm so cold
Let me in your window
Heathcliff, it's me, I'm Cathy
I've come home, I'm so cold."

17. What Irish singing trio had a hit single with "The Sound of Silence" in 1966?

18. What writing team wrote "Reach Out, I'll Be There ", a number 1 hit for the Four Tops in 1966?

19. Who wrote "Eloise", a hit for Barry Ryan in 1968?

20. Who played bass guitar on the Temptations hit "My Girl"?

Bonus Question:
In what year was "Return to Sender" by Elvis Presley a hit single?

QUIZ NUMBER 49

1. In what year was "Dedicated to the One I Love "by The Mamas and the Papas a hit single?

2. What group was Mike D'Abo lead singer with before he joined Manfred Mann?

3. Was "Everlasting Love" a number 1 hit single for Love Affair in 1968 or 1969?

4. "Bat Out of Hell" was a 1978 hit album for who?

5. "Live at Leeds" was a live album for what group?

6. Who wrote, "Albatross ", a number 1 hit single for Fleetwood Mac in January 1969?

7. "Madman Across the Water" was a 1971 album by what singer/songwriter?

8. Steve Harley and Cockney had a top ten hit single in 1976 with what Beatles song?

9. "No Milk Today" was a hit single for what group in 1966?

10. John Denvir's "Leaving on a Jet Plane" was a hit single for what trio in 1969?

11. What singer/songwriter had the 1972 hit single, "American Pie"?

12. Who was the drummer with 10cc from its inception until he departed the group in 1976?

13. Who sang lead vocals on "Lady Eleanor," by Lindisfarne?

14. Who was lead singer with The Pretty Things?

15. "Torn Between Two Lovers" was a hit single in 1977 by what singer?

16. What is Gilbert O'Sullivan's birth forename?

17. "Everything's Tuesday" was a 1971 hit single for what group?

18. "Was "Yellow River" by Christie a number 1 hit single in 1969 or 1970?

19. From what number 1 hit single do the following lyrics appear?
"I've seen all your qualifications
You got from the Sorbonne
And the painting you stole from Picasso
Your loveliness goes on and on, yes, it does
When you go on your summer vacation
You go to Juan-les-Pins."

20. "Behind a Painted Smile" was a 1969 hit single for what group?

Quiz 49 Bonus Question:
In the hit single in 1968 by singer, O.C. Smith, whose wife was described as "The Greatest Mom on Earth"?

QUIZ NUMBER 50

1. "Innervisions" was a 1973 hit album for what singer/songwriter?

2. "Come Tomorrow" was a 1965 hit single for what group?

3. David Harman was lead singer from what 1960's prolific hit making group?

4. What was the Troggs only number 1 hit single?

5. "Our Day Will Come" was a 1963 single release by what act?

6. "Tears of a clown" was a 1970 number 1 hit single for what act?

7. "I Saw Her Again" was a top ten hit for what group in 1966?

8. From what number 1 hit single do the following lyrics appear?
"You thought you was a clever girl (clever girl)
Giving up your social whirl (social whirl)
You can't come back and be the first in line, oh yeah
You're obsolete, my baby
My poor, unfaithful baby."

9. "Mine For Me", written by Paul McCartney, was on what Rod Stewart album?

10. Who was lead guitarist with Led Zeppelin?

11. "Poor Man's Son" was a 1965 hit single for what group?

12. How many top 20 hit singles did Barry McGuire have in the 1960's?

13. What was the last number 1 hit single for T Rex?

14. Who sang lead vocals on Chicago 's number 1 hit single, "If You Leave Me Now."?

15. "Brand New Key" was a hit single for who in 1971/1972?

16. Peter Skellern had a top ten hit single in 1972 with, "You're a – ". What's the missing word in the song's title?

17. "Face the Music" was a 1975 album by what progressive group?

18. What group had a 1975 hit album called "The Original Soundtrack."?

19. Who wrote "MacArthur Park "a hit for Richard Harris in 1968?

20. "Reflections of my Life" was a 1969 hit single for what group?

Quiz 50 Bonus Question:
What guitarist played lead fuzz guitar on the Carpenters hit, "Goodbye to Love "?

Quiz 51 Bonus Question:

Brian Ferry recorded a "Covers" album in 1973. Can you name it?

QUIZ NUMBER 52

1. "Heaven Must Have Sent You" was a number 3 hit single in 1971 by what group?

2. What was Slade's first number 1 hit single?

3. "Young Americans" was a hit single and album by what singer/songwriter?

4. The Overlanders had a number 1 hit single with The Beatles, "Michelle." What duo also had a top 20 hit with the song simultaneously in 1966?

5. "I've Got You Under My Skin" was a top 20 hit single in 1966 by what group?

6. "Don't Give Up - - "was a number 1 hit single for David Soul in 1977. Can you complete the song's title?

7. From what classic hit do the following lyrics appear?
"She takes the taxi to the good hotel
Bon marché as far as she can tell
She drinks the zombie from the cocoa shell
She feels alright, she get it on tonight, yeah."

8. What does the (J) stand for in Billy J Kramer?

9. What year did The Supremes have the hit, "Stop! In the Name of Love."?

10. "Empty Sky" is the debut album by what singer/songwriter in 1969?

11. What was Chuck Berry's final top 10 single in the 1960's?

12. What group had a 1970 hit single with, "Vehicle"?

13. "Can't You See That - -"was a top 10 hit single for the Dave Clark Five. Can you complete the song's title?

14. "Part of the Union" was a hit single for what group in 1973?

15. What was 10cc's last album before Godley and Creme left the group?

16. "Happy Jack" was a 1967 hit single for what group?

17. Who was lead singer with the Boomtown Rats?

18. What killed the radio star according to the Buggles in their 1979 hit?

19. "Sweet Baby James" was a hit album for what singer/songwriter in 1971?

20. "The Price of Love" was a 1965 hit single for what duo?

Bonus Question:
"She's About a Mover "and "Wooly Bully" were both hit singles in 1965, but which group had the hit, "Wooly Bully"?

ANSWERS
SECTION

QUIZ NUMBER 1

1. The Rolling Stones
2. Elton John
3. Frank Sinatra
4. You
5. Band of Gold
6. Jasamine in 1968
7. The Kinks
8. Paul McCartney
9. "Vincent" by Don McLean
10. Michael Jackson
11. Paul Kossoff
12. One. "I Heard it Through the Grapefruit" in 1969
13. Kiki Dee
14. Don Williams
15. Memphis
16. Eric Stewart
17. "All I Really Want to Do."
18. David Cassidy
19. "Ha Ha"
20. David Bowie

Bonus Answer

The Kinks. Peter Quaife was born with the surname, Kinnes, after his mother fell pregnant during the war to an American serviceman called Kinnes. The airman left for home shortly after the baby was born. The unmarried mother then married a man with the surname, Quaife and the boy was given his surname.

QUIZ NUMBER 2

1. I

2. The Who

3. "Tired of Waiting"

4. Gladys Knight

5. Apple

6. 1966

7. "Bohemian Rhapsody"

8. 10

9. Stevie Wonder

10. Sandie Shaw

11. Andrew Gold

12. "Everlasting Love"

13. Chi-Lites

14. David Bowie

15. Mike Smith

16. "Blackberry Way" a number 1 hit for the Move in 1969. "See My Baby Jive" and "Angel Fingers" both number 1 hits for Wizzard in 1973.

17. Sweet

18. The Beach Boys

19. Mark Knopfler

20. No. His biggest hit was "Back Off Boogaloo" a number 2 hit single in 1972.

Bonus Question

"Funny Familiar Forgotten Feelings"

QUIZ NUMBER 3

1. Polly Brown
2. Creedence Clearwater Revival
3. Harper's Bizarre
4. The Light
5. John Lennon's Plastic Ono Band
6. Maggie May
7. Ray Charles
8. James Taylor
9. Pink Floyd
10. Revolver
11. Slade
12. Jimmy Page
13. 1969
14. Reservation
15. George Martin
16. The Applejacks
17. The Herd
18. Abba
19. Easy
20. "Sha La La"

Bonus Question
Thirty-six different songs

QUIZ NUMBER 4

1. Supertramp
2. "She'd Rather Be with Me" in 1967
3. The Boomtown Rats
4. Gerry Goffin and Carole King
5. Donny Osmond

6. "In The Summertime", a number 1 hit single for Mungo Jerry in 1970.

7. Mulberry

8. The Monkees

9. The Street

10. Badfinger

11. No. The double (A) sided hit only reached number 3 in the charts.

12. Les Gray

13. "My Rose"

14. The Sex Pistols

15. Amen Corner

16. "Four in the morning"

17. Paul Weller

18. Tony Christie and R Dean Taylor

19. 1941

20. The Mersey

Bonus Answer
Denny Laine

QUIZ NUMBER 5

1. Chris Montez

2. Danger

3. David Bowie

4. Frank Allen

5. Jimi Hendrix

6. Lee Dorsey

7. None

8. "I Heard it Through the Grapevine".

9. Dreadlock

10. The Beach Boys

11. Seven
12. The Devil
13. Marianne Faithful
14. The Rubetts
15. 76 trombones plus Julie Driscoll, Brian Auger, and the trinity, which is five, plus Dawn's "knock 3 times", Len Barry had the hit, "1,2,3", which equals 6, plus Pete Wingfield's "18 With a Bullet". Total =108
16. A Clown
17. No
18. Status Quo
19. George Harrison
20. Desmond Dekker and the Aces

Bonus Answer
"Sweet Talking Woman"

QUIZ NUMBER 6
1. Ronnie Scott
2. The Doors
3. Amen Corner
4. Joe Walsh
5. "You Keep Me Hanging On"
6. Elvis Costello and The Attractions
7. Mott the Hoople
8. Shuffle
9. Positively 4th Street
10. Roberta Flack
11. Phil Spector
12. Pilot
13. Frankie Valli
14. Brian Ferry

15. I Can't Let Maggie Go
16. Jim Reeves
17. Slade
18. Dave Berry
19. The Stylistics
20. The Tams

Bonus Answer
i) Sweets for My Sweets
ii) The Drifters
iii) The Searchers

QUIZ NUMBER 7
1. The Four Tops
2. The Hollies
3. My Girl
4. Ian Drury and the Blockheads
5. Dave Dee, Dozy, Beaky, Mick, and Tich
6. Out of the Blue
7. Paul Jones
8. Paul Simon
9. The Carpenters
10. Noel Harrison
11. Elusive
12. 83
13. Klaus Voorman
14. O. C. Smith
15. Randy Edleman
16. Yes, it was.
17. Dave Edmunds
18 Glasgow
19. Rod Stewart

20. Burt Bacharach and Hal David

Bonus Answer
Ricky Nelson

QUIZ NUMBER 8
1. Chuck Berry
2. Bobby Vee
3. The Move
4. The Temptations
5. "Something in the Air" by Thunderclap Newman
6. Booker T and the M.G.s
7. Feargal Sharkey
8. Tommy
9. Asher and Waller
10. Chairmen of the Board
11. Rod Allen
12. Bev Bevan
13. The Eagles
14. Ozzy Osbourne
15. Supertramp
16. Newcastle
17. Abba
18. Paul Simon
19. All Things Must Pass
20. 1971

Bonus Answer
The Small Faces

QUIZ NUMBER 9
1. Levi Stubbs
2. Clodagh Rogers
3. Breakfast in America
4. The Beach Boys
5. Pilot
6. Cindy Birdsong
7. Ronnie Wood
8. Fleetwood Mac
9. Smokey Robinson and the Miracles
10. Ginger Baker
11. No, the highest position the song reached was number two.
12. Eric Stewart
13. You'll Never Walk Alone
14. T Rex
15. Mitch Mitchell
16. Bob Dylan's "Like a Rolling Stone"
17. Revolver
18. Christie
19. The Boomtown Rats
20. Elvis Presley

Bonus Answer
Skeeter Davis

QUIZ NUMBER 10
1. Chris Montez
2. The Sex Pistols
3. Alone
4. Lou Christie
5. Rita Coolidge

6. Dr Hook and the Medicine Show
7. John Entwistle
8. Pete Wingfield
9. Paul Rogers
10. 10 cc
11. Karen and Richard
12. 1967
13. Jimi Hendrix Experience
14. Rod Stewart
15. Debbie Harry
16. No
17. Leo Sayer
18. "You Were it Well".
19. Jim Reeves
20. Boy

Bonus Answer
Nothing Rhymed

QUIZ NUMBER 11
1. Paul McCartney
2. Boz Scaggs
3. Yes, in 1971
4. Crosby, Stills, Nash, and Young
5. Al Jardine
6. The Four Pennies
7. Don Powell
8. "You Really Got Me"
9. Elkie Brooks
10. 1967
11. Gilbert O'Sullivan
12. "Let the Heartaches Begin" in 1967

152

13. What's Going On
14. Dean Ford
15. Oliver's Army.
16. Tommy Roe
17. Terry Jacks
18. George Harrison and Ringo Srarr
19. Emerson, Lake, and Palmer
20. West Side Story

Bonus Answer

The Group was Honeybus. The song was "I Can't Let Maggie Go"

QUIZ NUMBER 12
1. Mind
2. Donovan
3. The Rubettes
4. Hey Jude
5. This Old Heat of Mine
6. Rod Stewart
7. Roy Wood
8. Green Tambourine
9. Ian Hunter
10. "Help!"
11. Jean Terrell
12. Rose Royce
13. Cat Stevens
14. 10cc
15. Amen Corner
16. Blondie
17. Joe Walsh
18. Sailor

19. Reg Presley
20. Paris

Bonus Answer
"Down Down" in 1975

QUIZ NUMBER 13
1. The Monkees
2. Smokie
3. Soho
4. Andrew Gold
5. Good Morning Starshine
6. Band on the Run
7. Stevie Wonder
8. Gerry and the Pacemakers
9. Wild Thing
10. Rod Stewart
11. The Carpenters
12. The Turtles
13. Ruby Tuesday
14. 10 CC
15. The Union Gap
16. 1962
17. Roger Taylor
18. Flowers
19. American Pie
20. Burt Bacharach and Hal David

Bonus Answer
The Bedrocks

QUIZ NUMBER 14

1. Blind Faith
2. One. "All or Nothing" in 1966
3. 1970
4. "Waterloo" in 1974
5. Jeff Lynne
6. The Strawbs
7. Wild World
8. John Lennon
9. Pink Floyd
10. R Dean Taylor
11. Frankie Valli
12. The Moody Blues
13. Love Affair
14. George Harrison
15. Donovan
16. Clem Burke
17. Mickey Dolenz
18. Rod Stewart
19. Judy Clay
20. Faces

Bonus Answer
"Goat's Head Soup" in 1973

QUIZ NUMBER 15

1. The Who
2. Bobby Vee
3. Love Hearts
4. Bob Dylan
5. Bruce Springsteen
6. Kenney Jones

7. Penny Lane
8. Myself
9. Maggie May
10. The Moon
11. Bread
12. Mick Avory
13. Annie Lennox
14. Tom Jones
15. 1967
16. David Bowie
17. Love Affair
18. Robert Plant
19. Ob La Di Ob La Da
20. Francis Rossi

Bonus Answer
"Little Red Rooster" by the Rolling Stones in December 1964

QUIZ NUMBER 16
1. Eight
2. Jim Reeves
3. The Tams
4. Bass Guitar
5. Mardi Gras
6. The Band
7. She Loves You
8. The Bellamy Brothers
9. "Baby Come Back" in 1968
10. Paul Weller
11. Peter Green
12. David Bowie

13. The Isley Brothers
14. Bridge Over Troubled Water
15. Ronnie Wood
16. Nina Simone
17. Lee Dorsey
18. Noel Redding
19. Alice Cooper
20. Procol Harum

Bonus Answer
"Massachusetts (The Lights Went Out In)."

QUIZ NUMBER 17
1. Bob Dylan
2. Paul McCartney
3. Carole Bayer Sager
4. Marmalade
5. Roy Wood
6. (If Paradise Is) Half as Nice
7. Rubber Bullets by 10 cc
8. Eyes
9. Yes
10. The Alan Price Set
11. Gary Leeds
12. Diana Ross
13. Pink Floyd
14. "24 Hours from Tulsa" in 1964
15. Carl Wilson
16. Gilbert O'Sullivan
17. Sue
18. Errol Brown
19. Them

20. Jim Webb

Bonus Answer
"Annie" in 1974

QUIZ NUMBER 18
1. David Gates
2. Mike Oldfield
3. Herman's Hermits
4. Away
5. Johnny Nash
6. Hotel California
7. The Bee Gees
8. Roger Miller
9. 10 cc
10. John Deacon
11. Knock Three Times
12. "If I Needed Someone"
13. The Kinks
14. Charlie Rich
15. The Moody Blues
16. Dave Cousins
17. The Seekers
18. Thieves
19. Don't Go Breaking My Heart
20. Frankie Valli

Bonus Answer
Demis Roussos with "The Roussos Phenomenon" in July 1976. He was born to Greek parents in 1946 in Alexandria, Egypt.

QUIZ NUMBER 19
1. The Doors
2. "Hello Goodbye" in 1967
3. 10 cc
4. Chip Hawkes
5. Marc Bolan
6. Thunderclap Newman
7. Good Vibrations
8. Paul Simon
9. Black is Black
10. Queen
11. Blue Mink
12. Bob Geldof
13. Eric Stewart
14. The Commodores
15. Barry
16. 1969
17. Frank Sinatra
18. Virginia Plain
19. Muswell Hill
20. Bruce Springsteen

Bonus Answer
June Carter Cash

QUIZ NUMBER 20
1. The Police
2. The Ivy League
3. Vision
4. Silence is Golden
5. Mott the Hoople
6. Bob Dylan

7. T Rex
8. Genesis
9. I Feel Fine
10. Dancing
11. The Bee Gees
12. The Searchers
13. The Tremeloes
14. The Walker Brothers
15. Billy Ocean
16. Ronnie 'Plonk' Lane
17. Paul McCartney
18. Waterloo
19. Donny Osmond
20. Mick Jagger and Keith Richards

Bonus Answer
High Time

QUIZ NUMBER 21
1. Teacup
2. "Hit the Road Jack" by Ray Charles
3. "The Wall" in 1979
4. Eddie Cochran
5. Squeeze
6. Chris Rea
7. Tony Orlando
8. 1964
9. Sparks
10. Shel Talmy
11. The Eagles
12. "Where Did Our Love Go" in 1964
13. Electric Light Orchestra

14. Michelle
15. Rod Stewart
16. "Wild Thing" in 1966
17. Elton John
18. Kenney Jones
19. Brian Connolly
20. Long John Baldry

Bonus Answer
Marvin Gaye

QUIZ NUMBER 22
1. Stevie Wonder
2. Peter Sarstedt
3. Elton John
4. "Homeward Bound" By Simon & Garfunkel
5. Noddy Holder
6. Abbey Road
7. Frankie Valli
8. Honeybus
9. Ray Dorset
10. Marmalade
11. EL0
12. Georgie Fame
13. Glen Campbell and Bobby Gentry
14. Bob Dylan
15. The Rolling Stones
16. The Real Thing
17. "Ruby Don't Take Your Love to Town" by Kenny Rogers and the First Edition
18. Elvis Costello
19. 1965

20. "Keep on Running" in 1966

Bonus Answer
"Can't Buy Me Love" in 1964

QUIZ NUMBER 23
1. Bruce Springsteen
2. Gerry Goffin and Carole King
3. The New Christie Minstrels
4. "Paperback Writer"
5. No. The writer has said in several interviews that he and his father always had a great relationship.
6. Gary Brooker
7. The Rolling Stones
8. Frank Allen
9. Smokie
10. Dave Dee, Dozy, Beaky, Mick, and Tich
11. Hot Chocolate
12. Night
13. The Four Tops
14. Pink Floyd
15. Graham Gouldman
16. Bohemian Rhapsody
17. Phil Collins
18. Leo Sayer
19. Robin Gibb
20. Justin Hayward

Bonus Answer
Wonderlove

QUIZ NUMBER 24

1. The Rolling Stones
2. "Vincent" by Don McLean
3. Burt Bacharach and Hal David
4. John Denver
5. Amen Corner
6. Showwaddywaddy
7. Sabre Dance
8. Craft
9. Tom Fogerty
10. The Righteous Brothers
11. Curtis Mayfield
12. Peter Sarstedt
13. Sam Cooke
14. The Beatles
15. Jethro Tull
16. Cliff Bennett and the Rebel Rousers
17. Debbie Harry
18. Keith West
19. Stevie Wonder
20. "Concrete and Clay" a number one hit for Unit 4 Plus Two

Bonus Answer
Klaus Voorman

QUIZ NUMBER 25

1. Ace
2. Joni Mitchell
3. Steve Marriott
4. The Stylistics

5. "Paint it Black" a number 1 hit for the Rolling Stones in 1966

6. The Four Tops

7. Judge

8. John Lennon

9. Squeeze

10. The Moody Blues

11. Melanie

12. Cupid's Inspiration

13. "MacArthur Park

14. Sonja Kristina

15. Billy Preston on "Get Back" and its (B) Side "Don't Let Me Down."

16. The Chi-Lites

17. "Of The Movies"

18. Wayne Fontana

19. ELO

20. Keith Relf

Bonus Answer

Session Drummer, Bobby Graham

QUIZ NUMBER 26

1. Faces

2. Elvis Presley

3. Pete Wingfield

4. George Harrison with "My Sweet Lord" in early 1971

5. The Troggs

6. "Lazy Sunday" a hit for The Small Faces in 1968

7. The Police

8. Kenny Rogers and the First Edition

9. From members, Tom McGuinness, and Hughie Flint

10. Mickey Dolenz
11. No. Mike D'Abo was.
12. John Lennon
13. Traffic
14. Blues
15. "Number 1"
16. The Shadows
17. 10 cc
18. "Green, Green Grass of Home" by Tom Jones
19. The Tom Robinson Band
20. "Melting Pot"

Bonus Answer
Led Zeppelin, from "Led Zeppelin II" in 1970, through "Led Zeppelin III, also 1970, "Led Zeppelin IV" in 1971 and "Houses of the Holy" 1973

QUIZ NUMBER 27
1. Rick Wakeman
2. Junior Campbell
3. "Everything I Own"
4. Steve Ellis
5. Redbone
6. Gerry Rafferty
7. Mama Told Me Not to Come
8. Eric Stewart
9. Andy Fairweather Low
10. Status Quo
11. Pearly Spencer
12. Crystal Gale
13. Sandie Shaw
14. Without You

15. Alan Price
16. The Wailers
17. 1965
18. Justin Hayward
19. Canada
20. Don Henley

Bonus Answer
The Echoes

QUIZ NUMBER 28
1. Peter and Gordon
2. Judith Durham
3. 1969
4. Actors, Terence Stamp, and Julie Christie
5. Slowhand
6. 1966
7. Van Morrison
8. Beatles for Sale
9. Peter Frampton
10. Yes, they were twins.
11. Scott Walker, real name, Noel Scott Engel
12. Kevin Godley
13. Christine Perfect
14. Sunny Afternoon
15. Johnny Nash
16. Stevie Wonder
17. Jackie Trent.
18. Wizzard featuring, Roy Wood.
19. Eleanor Rigby
20. Racing Cars

Bonus Answer

Leo Sayer. His manager at the time, Adam Faith, achieved the same feat from 1959 to 1961.

QUIZ NUMBER 29

1. Bye Bye Baby
2. Roberta Flack
3. Paul McCartney and Wings
4. No
5. David Paton
6. Jimmy Webb
7. Classical Gas
8. Crosby, Stills, Nash, and Young
9. The New Seekers
10. Jennie C Riley
11. Birmingham
12. Janis Ian
13. The Searchers. Frank Allen replaced him.
14. Denny Doherty
15. The Seekers
16. Faces
17. The Temptations
18. Perry Como
19. Reginald Dwight
20. London

Bonus Answer

Peter Cetera

QUIZ NUMBER 30

1. No. The 1974 hit, "The Air That I Breathe" only reached number two in the charts

2. Gilbert O'Sullivan

3. Misunderstood

4. Johnny Bristol

5. Humble Pie

6. T Rex. "Electric Warrior"- "Prophets, Seers, and Sages/My People Were Fair"- and "Bolan Boogie" in 1972.

7. John Fogerty

8. "Don't Let it Die" by Hurricane Smith

9. Yesterday

10. David Essex

11. Marvin Gaye

12. Rose Royce

13. The Monkees

14. Teddy Pendergrass

15. Arnold Layne

16. Status Quo with 106 performances.

17. The Dave Clark Five

18. Bobby Darin

19. 1963

20. When I Grow Up to Be a Man

Bonus Answer

Harry Nillson

QUIZ NUMBER 31

Hit Singles of 1966

1. The Walker Brothers

2. The Toys

3. My Girl
4. Herb Alpert and the Tijuana Band
5. The Four Seasons
6. The Overlanders
7. Day
8. Barbara Streisand
9. Len Barry
10. Mirror Mirror
11. Cilla Black
12. The Animals
13. No. It reached number 3 in the charts.
14. The Yardbirds
15. Eddie Arnold
16. Shotgun Wedding
17. Steve Marriott and Ronnie Lane
18. Pretty Flamingo
19. Getaway
20. Gerry Goffin and Carole King

Bonus Answer
Gene Pitney

QUIZ NUMBER 32
1960'S Albums
1. The Mamas and the Papas
2. Nat King Cole
3. Home
4. The Rolling Stones
5. Pet Sounds
6. The Doors
7. Simon & Garfunkel
8. Big Brother and the Holding Company
9. The Who

10. Creedence Clearwater Revival
11. Elvis Presley
12. Simon & Garfunkel
13. Johnny Cash
14. River
15. Van Morrison
16. The Doors
17. The Jimi Hendrix Experience
18. The Rolling Stones
19. Coupe
20. Andy Williams in 1963.

Bonus Answer
"Blonde on Blonde" in 1966

QUIZ NUMBER 33
1. Pete Townsend of The Who produced "Something in the Air," a number one single for Thunderclap Newman in 1969
2. Marvin Gaye
3. Phil Coulter
4. Tony Orlando and Dawn
5. Dave Davies
6. Baby
7. "Help!"
8. George Harrison
9. The Four Seasons
10. The Sex Pistols
11. Bill Wyman, born on the 24th of October 1936
12. "Teaser and the Firecat"
13. The Paper Dolls
14. The Beach Boys
15. The Everly Brothers

16. Odyssey
17. Cliff Richard
18. The Carpenters
19. Medicine Head
20. Roxy Music

Bonus Answer
"The Scotch of St James club" in London.

QUIZ NUMBER 34
1. Joe South
2. 1966
3. Junior Campbell
4. Mike D'Abo and Tony Macaulay
5. T Rex
6. "Baby You're a Rich Man"
7. Brian Connolly
8. Jack Jones
9. "How Dare You" in 1976.
10. 1967
11. Don Henley and Glen Frey
12. "Something" in 1969
13. A New World Record
14. The Dixie Cups
15. Egg
16. Traffic
17. Stevie Wonder
18. Bright Eyes
19. "With a Little Help from My Friends"
20. The Carpenters

Bonus Answer
"S.O.S" by Abba

QUIZ NUMBER 35
1. The Tams
2. Jackie De Shannon
3. Nigel
4. Please Mr Postman
5. The Eagles
6. Tea For the Tillerman
7. Cream
8. Billy Joel
9. Bob Dylan
10. Paul McCartney and Wings
11. Eight
12. Nothing Rhymed
13. The Small Faces
14. Songs in the Key of Life
15. "Baby Love", a number 1 hit single for the Supremes in 1964
16. Neil Sedaka
17. Cream
18. Mississippi
19. Fleetwood Mac
20. "Without You" by Nilsson

Bonus Answer
Steve Winwood

QUIZ NUMBER 36
1. Twice as Much
2. Band on the Run
3. The Fortunes
4. Slade
5. Junior Campbell

6. Pillow
7. Roy Wood
8. Al Green
9. ELO
10. Elvis Costello
11. Autumn Almanac
12. Blondie
13. Boz Scaggs
14. "The Beatles" AKA "The White Album" in 1968
15. "Here Comes the Night" by Them
16. Sweet
17. The Move
18. Roger Whittaker
19. Gun
20. The Three Degrees

Bonus Answer

Black Sabbath. "Hotel California" was partly recorded at the Criteria Studios, Miami where Black Sabbath were recording their album "Technical Ecstasy" at the same time. Such was the din from the English group that noise from their studio leaked through to the adjoining studio making it impossible for the Eagles to record their song.

QUIZ NUMBER 37
1. Peter Noone
2. Dave Dee, Dozy, Beaky, Mick, and Tich
3. Mark Feld
4. Gin House
5. The Blue Flames
6. One. "Silence is Golden" in 1967
7. No, his brother John was.

8. John Phillips
9. 1967
10. John Leyton
11. Proud Mary
12. "Games People Play" in 1969
13. "Something's Gotten Hold of My Heart."
14. Roger Cook and Roger Greenaway
15. The Showstoppers
16. The Rolling Stones
17. Plastic Ono Band
18. Art Garfunkel
19. "It Must Be Him"
20. They were brothers. Kane's real name is Richard Sarstedt

Bonus Answer
Bobby Darin

QUIZ NUMBER 38
1. Paul McCartney
2. The Clash
3. Wings
4. Crosby, Stills, Nash, and Young
5. Al Jardine
6. The Four Pennies
7. Levon Helm
8. You Really Got Me
9. Elkie Brooks
10. The Tremeloes
11. Gilbert O'Sullivan
12. Let the Heartaches Begin
13. What's Going On

14. Dean Ford
15. "Oliver's Army" by Elvis Costello
16. Tommy Roe
17. Terry Jacks
18. George Harrison and Ringo Starr
19. Chic
20. West Side Story

Bonus Answer

The group was Honeybus. The hit was "I Can't Let Maggie Go."

QUIZ NUMBER 39
1. Marvin Gaye
2. Reparta and the Delrons
3. Johnny Nash
4. Elton John
5. The Bachelors
6. Leo Sayer
7. Summer in the City
8. 1976
9. The Rockin' Berries
10. Brian Ferry
11. 1977
12. Herman's Hermits
13. The Real Thing
14. "Blackberry Way" in February 1969
15. Shawaddywaddy
16. The Supremes
17. Hammer
18. Don Henley
19. The Equals
20. The Show Must Go On

Bonus Answer

In 1976 Cat Stevens almost drowned off the coast of Malibu. He shouted, "Oh, God if you save me, I will work for you." Almost immediately a wave carried him back to shore. This brush with death intensified his long-held quest for spiritual truth.

QUIZ NUMBER 40

1. This Wheel's on Fire
2. The Bee Gees
3. Fleetwood Mac
4. Billy Joel
5. The Show Must Go On
6. Wayne Fontana
7. Stevie Wonder
8. Denny Laine
9. But My Love
10. Manfred Mann
11. James Taylor
12. David Bowie
13. Darling
14. Lynn Anderson
15. I Can't Explain
16. Blondie
17. Paul McCartney and Wings
18. Life
19. Dr Feelgood
20. The Tremeloes

Bonus Answer

Terry Kath

QUIZ NUMBER 41
1. Donny Osmond
2. Barry McGuire who had a 1965 hit single with "Eve of Destruction".
3. David Gates' "Everything I Own"
4. The Boomtown Rats
5. Rita Coolidge
6. Roger Taylor
7. The Who
8. Blondie
9. Ian Anderson
10. Nancy Sinatra and Lee 'Boots' Hazelwood
11. "Waterloo Sunset" wasn't a number 1 hit single. It reached number 2 in the charts in 1967.
12. Rod Stewart
13. Donovan
14. "I'm A Boy" by The Who
15. Joan Baez
16. Jim Reeves
17. Ralph McTell
18. Get Down
19. 1968
20. Away

Bonus Answer
John Maus, who changed his name to John Walker when he became a member of the Walker Brothers.

QUIZ NUMBER 42
1. Mickey Most
2. Eden Kane
3. The Rockin' Berries

4. "Paperback Writer"
5. Status Quo
6. The Jimi Hendrix Experience
7. John Rowles
8. A paper bag.
9. Peter York
10. "A Whiter Shade of Pale"
11. "Beatles for Sale" released in late 1964.
12. Cher
13. "My Cherie Amour
14. Eddie Grant
15. Ginger Baker
16. 1977
17. Andrew Gold
18. The Who
19. Rod Stewart
20. Gordon Sumner AKA Sting

Bonus Answer
The Righteous Brothers

QUIZ NUMBER 43
1. Freddie Mercury
2. Tony Crane
3. Johnny Kidd and The Pirates
4. "Reach Out, I'll Be There" by The Four Tops
5. The Fortunes
6. Nancy Sinatra
7. Tony Hicks
8. Stephen Stills
9. 1968
10. Keith Relf

11. Paradise

12. "Crying in the Chapel" in 1965.

13. "Dedicated Follower of Fashion" a hit for The Kinks.

14. Neil Sedaka

15. Tom McGuinness

16. Bev Bevan

17. The Troggs

18. Two…. "It's Not Unusual" in 1965 and "The Green Green Grass of Home" in 1966/1967.

19. Status Quo

20. The Four Seasons

Bonus Answer

Session musician, Big Jim Sullivan played guitar on all the songs mentioned.

QUIZ NUMBER 44

1. The Rolling Stones

2. The Jimi Hendrix Experience

3. Chris Norman

4. "Just Like a Woman" in 1966

5. Suzie Quatro

6. The Hollies. They got the title from Alan Clark's wife's forename and Graham Nash's then wife's surname.

7. Billy Joel

8. "Oh, Pretty Woman", a number 1 hit for Roy Orbison in 1964

9. The Shadows

10. Remember

11. Squeeze

12. Hair
13. Songs in the Key of Life
14. "Eleanor" in 1968
15. Donna Summer
16. "Mr Tambourine Man" by The Byrds.
17. Little Red Book
18. The Young Rascals. The group dropped the 'Young' in 1968.
19. Roger Taylor
20. Norman

Bonus Answer
Dave Dee, Dozy, Beaky, Mick, and Tich

QUIZ NUMBER 45
1. Bob Dylan
2. Elkie Brooks
3. Pictures of "Matchstick Me
4. Steve Harley and Cockney Rebel
5. Nights in White Satin
6. Mardi Gras
7. Nina Simone
8. Blondie
9. One. "I'm Alive" in 1965.
10. Jethro Tull
11. John Phillips
12. Mungo Jerry
13. Dean Ford
14. Rod Stewart
15. Country
16. David Bowie
17. One. "Green Tambourine" in 1968.

18. "Just the Way You Are"
19. "Where Did Our Love Grow"
20. Sherbet

Bonus Answer
"Rat Trap" by The Boomtown Rats in 1978.

QUIZ NUMBER 46
What Year-Round
1. 1963
2. 1967
3. 1965
4. 1976
5. 1979
6. 1977
7. 1964
8. 1966
9. 1971
10. 1972
11. 1975
12. 1975
13. 1975
14. 1972
15. 1968
16. 1966
17. 1970
18. 1974
19. 1968
20. 1979

Bonus Answer
1976

QUIZ NUMBER 47
Girls! Girls! Girls!
1. Cilla Black
2. Marianne Faithful
3. Skeeter Davis
4. Cher
5. The Shangri-Las
6. 1960
7. 1964
8. Phil Spector
9. Captain of Your Ship
10. The Paper Dolls
11. Joni Mitchell
12. I Say a Little Prayer
13. Carly Simon
14. Stevie Nicks
15. Donna Summer
16. Carole King
17. Barbara Streisand
18. Diana Ross
19. Suzi Quatro
20. Twinkle

Bonus Answer
Abba

QUIZ NUMBER 48
1. T Rex
2. Don and Phil
3. Dino Danelli
4. Eve Graham and Lynn Paul
5. Goodbye Yellow Brick Road

6. The Walker Brothers
7. In a plane crash in 1997
8. George Harrison
9. Cliff Richard
10. Davy Jones
11. Andy Partridge
12. Charlie Rich
13. "Back to the Egg" In 1979
14. Ronnie Lane
15. Love
16. Wuthering Heights" by Kate Bush
17. The Bachelors
18. Holland/Dozier/Holland
19. His brother, Paul Ryan.
20. James Jamerson

Bonus Answer
1962

QUIZ NUMBER 49
1. 1967
2. A Band of Angels
3. 1968
4. Meatloaf
5. The Who
6. The group's lead guitarist and singer, Peter Green
7. Elton John
8. "Here Comes the Sun"
9. Herman's Hermits
10. Peter, Paul, and Mary
11. Don McLean
12. Kevin Godley

13. Alan Hull
14. Phil May
15. Mary MacGregor
16. Raymond
17. Chairmen of the Board
18. 1970
19. "Where Do You Go to My Lovely" by Peter Sarstedt in 1969.
20. The Isley Brothers

Bonus Answer
Hickory Hollis Tramp

QUIZ NUMBER 50
1. Stevie Wonder
2. Manfred Mann
3. Dave Dee, Dozy, Beaky, Mick, and Tich
4. "With a Girl Like You" in 1966.
5. Ruby and the Romantics
6. Smokey Robinson and the Miracles
7. The Mamas and the Papas
8. "Out of Time" by Chris Farlowe
9. Smiler
10. Jimmy Page
11. The Rockin' Berries
12. One. "Eve of Destruction" in 1965.
13. "Metal Guru" in 1972
14. Peter Cetera
15. Melanie
16. Lady
17. ELO
18. 10 cc

19. Jimmy Webb
20. Marmalade

Bonus Answer
Tony Peluso

QUIZ NUMBER 51
1. Chrispian St Peters
2. America
3. "Oh, No Not My Baby"
4. "You're My World" in 1964
5. Led Zeppelin
6. Tony Orlando
7. Scott Walker
8. She
9. The Kinks
10. Manhattan Transfer
11. The Four Seasons
12. Elvis Presley
13. He's Mistra Know It All" by Stevie Wonder
14. The Four Seasons
15. "Indiana Wants Me."
16. Traffic
17. Supertramp
18. The Funk Brothers
19. Sparks
20. Gilbert O'Sullivan

Bonus Answer
"These Foolish Things."

QUIZ NUMBER 52

1. The Elgins

2. "Cuz I Love You" in 1971.

3. David Bowie

4. David and Jonathan

5. The Four Seasons

6. "On Us"

7. "Haitian Divorce" by Steely Dan in 1976.

8. It doesn't stand for anything. John Lennon suggested Billy to use it as it sounded good!

9. 1965

10. Elton John

11. "No Particular Place to Go" in 1964

12. The Ides of March

13. "She's Mine"

14. The Strawbs

15. "How Dare You" in 1976

16. The Who

17. Bob Geldorf

18. Video

19. James Taylor

20. The Everly Brothers

Bonus Answer

Sam the Sham and the Pharaohs

Printed in Dunstable, United Kingdom

67692698R00107